Hallelujah Factor

by Jack R. Taylor

D1495316

Mansfield, PA

Dedication

This volume is lovingly and gratefully dedicated to the following:

My dad, Bob Taylor, whose serious illness was discovered during the time of this writing, and whose courage was a deeper motivation for me to do this work as quickly as possible. He knew the book would be dedicated to him, and we both had hoped he would live to see it finished. In God's greater wisdom Dad was taken to heaven in the midst of my work on this book. From where he is now, his perspective is glorious!

Alice Burkhart, my mother-in-law, who was taken suddenly and unexpectedly into the presence of God toward the end of this work. Her delightful sense of humor, her healing from emotional bondage, and her love for the Lord were sources of praise for us all.

The members of the body of Christ at Southcliff Baptist Church, Fort Worth, Texas, where many of these lessons on praise were delivered for the first time.

Those whose lives will be blessed as they put into action the principles of praise.

© Copyright 1983, 1999 by Jack Taylor
Revised and updated edition
All rights reserved

ISBN 1-883906-33-4

Kingdom Publishing
P.O. Box 486, Mansfield, PA 16933
(800) 597-1123 (570) 662-7515
http://www.kingdompub.com
email = info@kingdompub.com

Unless otherwise noted, all Scripture quotations are from HOLY BIBLE *New International Version,* copyright © 1978, New York Bible Society. Used by permission.

Hallelujah Factor

Table of Contents (Cont.)

The Factor: An Introduction

There is a *factor* in evangelical circles which we have all but forgotten.

What do I mean by *factor*? The dictionary discusses a factor as "any one of the causes of a result; one element in a situation."

The Church has been careful to take into consideration most of the factors in society which affect our ability to reach our generation with the Gospel of Christ. We have made our studies of population growth and future trends. We have considered the changing tastes and habits of our prospective constituency along with sociological or economic factors, cultural factors, racial factors, and a host of others.

We have built our church plants to facilitate the crowds and expose them to the Gospel within the framework of the most appealing and comfortable accommodations. We have organized all sorts of fellowships and arranged every conceivable means of togetherness to keep people from being lonely. We have utilized every available innovation to do the work more efficiently—we are experts on efficiency.

We have the latest in educational gadgets and are seeking to better understand the psychology of reaching people and appealing to them. We have seminars, retreats, advances, clutches (whatever they are), dialogues, sharing sessions, strategic meetings, colloquiums, and institutes *ad infinitum*. We talk of thrusts, motivation, mobilization, and implementation. We have the feeling that the latest meeting, the most recent innovation, the newest thrust is bound to be the ultimate scheme and will surely usher in the Kingdom of God.

But I call upon you to consider another factor so vital that I believe no method can succeed without it. The word *hallelujah*, as the reader will discover later, is an almost universal word for praise and is, in fact, the premier word for praise in the Bible. I have titled this book as a challenge for us to include the *praise factor* in the list of other factors being considered.

By all means consider all other pertinent factors in any issue. Leave out nothing which stands to have a possible effect on the outcome of any action; but, for the glory of God, be sure that this all-important factor is given due consideration!

Praise is not a peripheral or side factor, but is central and vital. One of the reasons for its centrality is this: it seeks the glory of God first of all. How sorely this is needed in the present age of self-centered subjectivism, when even evangelism and revival are sought on the basis of self-gratification.

The praise factor must be considered, not only for growth in quality and quantity of the Body of Christ, but in the area of the emotional well-being of the members in that Body. We need to be armed because our archenemy, the devil, has launched a major offensive in these days—possibly the last days.

I make a joyful prediction. The reader who takes to heart the truths of this book, and who employs and enjoys the high privilege and principles of praise, will be so blessed that the day will be marked as special on which he discovered the *Hallelujah Factor.*

Note to the Reader

The original edition (then called *The Hallelujah Factor*) began in August 1982, when the Southcliff Baptist Church of Fort Worth, Texas, asked me to serve as interim pastor. At first the thought of serving in that capacity seemed quite out of the question, my schedule being already full for the months following. However, I sought the Lord and His will for the matter, asking if perhaps He had a special word for the church. Above all of the impressions that crowded my mind, one stood out clearly. It seemed that the Lord was whispering to my heart, "I want my people to praise My Name." That inner impression soon prevailed, and during the next few days it was confirmed no less than *half a dozen times.* I accepted the position of interim pastor, making shifts in my schedule in order to preach as often as I could. However, my acceptance was contingent upon several stipulations: I would serve as interim pastor from August to December; I would preach upon nothing but praise; the church would itself adopt the theme of praise using two verses as the Scriptural focus. The first was Psalm 150:6, "Let everything that has breath praise the Lord." This was to be our *corporate* theme. The second was Psalm 119:164, "Seven times a day I praise you for your righteous laws." That was to be our *personal* theme.

The church voted in the affirmative, and I began a term as interim pastor that was to continue for 119 days. My commitment was to preach on praise for that entire period, but at that time I had only *one* sermon on the subject of praise. My first project was to take a new Bible, a *New International Version,* and mark each reference I found on the subject of praise. I was not surprised that there were frequent references to praise, but I was literally astounded by the number of them. The Bible came alive at the point of praise as never before. I was soon launched into a study and an adventure unprecedented in my previous thirty-five years of preaching ministry.

Although that period of preaching ended in 1983, my study and preaching on the subject of praise had only just begun. The response of Southcliff Baptist Church was encouraging and delightful. My own life was blessed beyond my power to describe. Many who participated testified to changed lives resulting from the study and practice of praise.

Now, more than 15 years later, Hallelujah Factor returns stronger than ever, thanks to the opportunity to reprint it in partnership with Kingdom Publishing. As we prepared this edition, they asked if there was any additional word I would like to share with the readers. Yes, there is. My experiences of the last 15 years have served to convince me even more of the power, purposes, and pleasure of praise and worship. In fact, I'd like to share with you the story of how praise actually saved my life.

In 1989, during a ministry trip, I suffered chest pains and found myself in a hospital, miles from home, facing heart surgery. The emergency nature of the situation precluded the possibility of returning home. The surgery went off without a problem, and I awakened in a total disposition of praise—which affected not only me but others as well.

At first, when the nurses awakened me in intensive care, I could not respond; but the calling of my name continued, from one nurse on the left and one on the right. I fully awakened in a room brighter than artificial light can render. I saw the faces of my nurses and flowers in the hall, and felt an unprecedented sense of the presence of God. I thought at the time that it was something only I was feeling, until one of the intensive care nurses came to visit me after I had gone to a private room. She had been the nurse at my right side calling for me to wake up. She shared that she, too, had sensed the presence of God and was changed.

I was released from the hospital after only 14 days, but the surgeon and cardiologist requested that I stay in the area for another week so that they could give me a final check-up before I went home. Accordingly, I arranged to stay at a resort about an hour from the hospital. While recuperating there, I suddenly experienced extreme and unrelieved pain. Upon readmission to the hospital, my heart surgeon announced that apparently, in the course of my first hospitalization, I had contracted a staph infection. Staph is serious wherever it is found, but it can be fatal when located anywhere near the heart. A second, far more serious surgery would be needed both to stem the infection and to repair the damage it had caused.

My experience after the second surgery was totally different. I awakened in what seemed like a dark pit. There was little if any light. I had tubes down my nose to my stomach, tubes inserted between my ribs on both sides, tubes into and out of my stomach. I was miserable. The morphine administered for pain caused frightening dreams, waking and sleeping. I began to sense a cloud of darkness descending upon me. In a few days, as my condition continued to worsen, a third surgery was necessitated by an infection along the incision line of the second surgery. This third surgery opened in my chest a cavity so fearfully large that it took me several days to work up the courage to look at it in the mirror!

Enduring three surgeries in twenty-one days was almost more than my physical and emotional frame could endure. To this point I had prayed, read the Bible, and even journaled in my quiet time. Now, the focus was on surviving. I lost a pound a day for 30 days as the staph infection raged in my body.

One night between the hours of midnight and three a.m., I had a profound experience with God. I was spent and in the most intense physical pain I have ever known. In my weakened state, God came to me with the thought that I could, by my own choice, ask Him and He would end it all. I could go home to heaven. I talked to God about this, and in a semiconscious state I experienced a renewed desire to live and to finish my earthly task. This experience marked the turning point of my 50 days in the hospital.

I was released after 72 days combined hospitalization and recuperation—from a city that I had initially planned to visit for just four days! I detoured to our lovely condominium on the Florida coast for thirty days of additional recuperation. Later, I returned once more to the place of my surgeries for more repair of my chest cavity.

For three and a half years after my multiple surgeries, I was introduced into a season of intermittent clinical depression. I did not ask for medication to alleviate this depression, nor did I desire it, although in retrospect it seems obvious that I could probably have had an easier time had I relented and received it. So I endured days of nightmarish dreams, awakening in the middle of the night with feelings of panic—clothing and bed saturated with sweat. Overwhelming feelings of guilt, shame, hopelessness and helplessness, worthlessness and wretchedness all held me in their vice-like grip. Trouble in the church where my son and I co-pastored accentuated the depression.

I have shared my experience to make this point: Had it not been for my practice of praise during this time, I do not believe I would have survived. When I was stabbed awake in the dead of night by a nightmare or panic attack, my long-practiced habits of praise served well. I would respond to these events by launching into a declaration of praises to God, particularly through the use of the compound names of God which are explored extensively in Chapter 5 of this book, "The Person We Praise." Many times I would continue to go through the several names for God, in a spirit of desperate praise, until I could win some ease and go back to sleep. This happened hundreds of times over a period of more than three years.

One day, in the third year, I walked slowly out of darkness into the sunshine of a day brighter than I had ever known. Praise continues to be a constant habit of my life. Does it work? Yes! Praise works because it releases God to work. It centralizes the greatness of God as expressed in the Father, the Son, and the Holy Spirit. It decentralizes self and the problems at hand, shoves self-absorbed feelings to an inferior position, and focuses instead on the eternal verities of our faith—our God reigns!

What you are about to read is a report of a fellow pilgrim on the adventurous journey of knowing the Sovereign God of the universe through His Son, Jesus Christ, our Lord, and by means of the inspiration and instruction of His Holy Spirit. I trust that the words on the following pages can somehow convey to you the complete captivation I experience with this study. Read it slowly. Stop at the end of the chapters and do the exercises I have labeled "Projects in Praise." Use the appendices for additional in-depth study and encouragement. Memorize the Scriptures. Set aside time each day as praise time. I feel safe in telling you that if you will engage in a serious study and practice of praise, your life will never be the same.

The Perspective of Praise

Give me a lever long enough and a place to stand and I will move the earth. —Archimedes

Leverage requires two things. First, there must be a reference for leverage: a fulcrum. Second, there must be an instrument of leverage. In relating to a dynamic philosophy of life, praise surely must be the lever, and the sovereignty of God must be the reference point. I want you to ponder that statement long enough to glimpse a praise perspective.

If praise is based upon elusive human hopes and is nothing more than a modified positive-thinking exercise, it is surely—among the follies of this world—the most futile.

But—if praise is a spontaneous response to the most mighty and powerful Truth, then we dare not live without it!

The fatalist can never praise the Lord, because the fatalist's underlying philosophy denies that life will come to any good or that, conversely, any good can come to life. The pessimist can never sing the songs of joy and praise; he simply does not have a supporting philosophy or perspective.

If this book were a building, this chapter would be the foundation. The building can be no sturdier than its foundation. Here I hope to lay a foundation upon which can be built a superstructure of praise for the life of the reader. The cornerstone of the foundation, throughout this book, will be God's Word.

In order to underline the importance of this concept, I'd like to suggest another metaphor: Any philosophy of praise must surely be built upon the sovereignty of God—our fulcrum. With God as our fulcrum and praise as our lever, we can indeed move the world into proper perspective.

Please note that although the conceptual aspects of praise

will dominate the first part of this book, practical exercises in praise will be offered at the close of every chapter.

Praise Defined

Let us use, as our working definition of praise, the following description: ***Praise is vocal, audible, and/or visible adoration of God.*** Throughout the chapters of this book, we will build upon this definition and refine it until finally, in Appendix A, we revisit the presuppositions upon which it is built.

Examining this further, we find in the Psalms, our chief source of references concerning praise and its exercise, that the practice of praise seems to be in three categories:

First, **praise may be vocal.** "My mouth will speak in praise of the Lord" (Psalm 145:21). In yet another instance the psalmist declares, "My lips will glorify you" (Psalm 63:3). In a number of verses we note that a shout is involved. "Shout with joy to God, all the earth!" (Psalm 66:1) Still another reference is that of "proclaiming aloud your praise" (Psalm 26:7). All of these verses reveal the *vocal* aspect of adoration.

However, **praise may be *audible* without being vocal.** Clapping is audible. "Clap your hands, all you nations" (Psalm 47:1*a*). Other means of audible praise are mentioned in Psalm 150:3-5. "Praise him with the sounding of the trumpet, praise him with the harp and lyre, praise him with the tambourine and dancing, praise him with the strings and flute, praise him with the clash of cymbals, praise him with resounding cymbals."

The third category involves cases where **praise may be neither vocal nor audible.** One is the lifting of the hands. "In your name I will lift up my hands," declared the psalmist in Psalm 63:4. (We will deal more extensively with this form of praise later when we examine the Hebrew words for praise.). Another form of praise that is neither vocal nor audible is *dancing.* David danced before the Lord when the ark was finally brought to its rightful place. The record reads, "So all Israel brought up the ark of the covenant of the Lord with shouts, with the sounding of rams' horns and trumpets, and of cymbals, and the playing of lyres and harps." As the ark of the covenant was entering the city of David, Michal, the daughter of Saul, watched from a window. And when she saw King David *dancing* in celebration, "she despised him in her heart" (1 Chronicles 15:28-29). David himself suggests in Psalm 149:3 "Let them praise his name with dancing."

Yet another form of praise that is visible, yet not audible or vocal, is that of *kneeling*. In fact, one of the words used in connection with this form of praise in the Old Testament is *havah*. It is used more than sixty times in Scripture and refers to a position of prostration or kneeling. It is generally translated *worship*. Some of the references in the Word to this form of praise are the following: 1 Chronicles 16:29 "Bring an offering and come before him; worship [*havah*] the Lord in the splendor of his holiness." 2 Chronicles 20:18: "Jehoshaphat bowed with his face to the ground, and all the people of Judah and Jerusalem fell down in worship [*havah*] before the Lord." Psalm 96:9 "Worship [*havah*] the Lord in the splendor of his holiness."

Clearly, the Old Testament people of faith practiced praise with their whole hearts. How about the New Testament believers?

John on Patmos Isle

For our current perspective on praise, turn to Revelation 4. John had, in his old age, suffered the ultimate rejection of his society for the testimony of Jesus Christ: He had been banished to the lonely Isle of Patmos to live out his remaining days. His surroundings offered no hope; his associates were those rejected by society. His remaining friends were far away, and weighing on his mind were the memories of hundreds of friends who had been called upon to make the supreme sacrifice of their lives for the sake of the Gospel.

If ever a man had reason to feel depressed, it was John on Patmos. The Church was being persecuted everywhere. It was unsafe to be a Christian in any part of the Roman Empire. The man who sat on the throne hated Christianity and seemed committed to wiping all Christians from the face of the earth.

It is at this dark moment in the life of John that we come to the vantage point of praise. John had just seen a vision of the glorified Christ. So different was He from what John *remembered* his Master to be that he dared not venture past the cautious observation that He was *"like* the Son of Man." This was no "lowly Savior, meek and mild." This was an imposing figure, with a voice like a hundred cascading waterfalls. His eyes flashed fire. His words were like a sharp sword. His feet were like burnished brass, speaking of judgment completed. He was dressed in a royal robe with a golden sash about His chest. His hair was white, and His face shone like the sun in its brilliance. He held seven stars in His right hand and walked among seven golden candlesticks.

In the vision, He explained His mission and ordered John to write the things which he had seen and heard. He then proceeded to dictate messages to the seven churches of Asia. Imagine the implications of the first three chapters of the Book of Revelation, in which Jesus reveals Himself, His interests, and His plans. Chapter four of the Revelation declares the underlying theme of all creation, giving us the perspective needed to engage in perpetual praise.

An Open Door

John said, "After this I looked, and there before me was a door standing open in heaven" (Revelation 4:1). The implication here is obvious. There is an open door between John and heaven. It is *purposely* open, suggesting the immediate possibility of entrance. Praise the Lord for such doors! In Revelation 1, John experienced two realms of reality. The first was the world of visible reality—that world was dark and filled with danger, offering no hope whatsoever. Suddenly John's eyes were enabled to view another world, the reality of the invisible. He states, "I was on the Isle of Patmos … on the Lord's day I was in the spirit." In this spiritual realm, he saw the reality of the invisible truth and faithfully reported it to us.

Like John, each of us is faced with these two realms of reality. All of our troubles with depression and hopelessness rise at the point of our conviction as to which realm is more real. We deal with the visible, the tangible, every day. We know that it is real. Bills must be paid. Sickness and death are a part of every man's lot. There are increasing fears, doubts, rejection, anxieties, and terrifying developments on the horizon which seem to threaten the very survival of the human race.

But there is another world, another realm of reality which beckons our attention: the spiritual, the heavenly, the eternal—the world of invisible spiritual reality. You and I tend to believe that this is foggy, misty, and unreal; yet as John realized on Patmos, this is true reality. After all, the ultimate test of reality is survival, and nothing we see, touch, taste, smell, or feel is indestructible. The tangible is always in the process of decay and simply will not survive the ultimate dismissal of time. *The invisible is the real.*

The door which John saw open was the door between earth and heaven, the aperture between the visible reality and the invisible (and genuine) reality. As we relive this experience with John, I want to challenge you to see the open door which is before *you* as well–a doorway into an *upside-down* kingdom!

A Voice in Heaven

In John's vision, the open door was soon accompanied by a trumpet-like voice which commanded, "Come up here and I will show you what must take place after this." (Revelation 4:1*b*).

John identified this voice as the same which had first spoken to him, the voice of Jesus Himself! Then there was an invitation. "Come up here," the Savior demanded. The door was open in heaven, and the very King of that spiritual reality issued the invitation to enter. Then came the explanation, "I will show you what must take place after this." Now we learn the key to history. Not only are there two realms of reality, the seen and the unseen, but *the unseen realm controls the seen.* We have thought it the other way around. This is the reason it has been difficult to have faith, *for faith's foundational claim is that real, genuine reality is in the area of the invisible.*

We could paraphrase what Jesus is saying to John: "Listen, things are not as they appear to be. They never are! I am about to show you things as they really are. I am about to walk you into the throne-room of the universe and show you genuine reality!"

In *The Upside-Down Kingdom*, Donald B. Kraybill describes Kingdom reality as "inverted or upside down when compared with the conventionally accepted values, norms, and relationships ..." He accurately describes the struggle we each face in trying to live in the spiritual reality while bound to this physical reality. "Kingdom ways of living do not mesh smoothly with the dominant society. In fact they may sometimes appear foolish." John was glimpsing through that doorway a kingdom *upside down* compared to this fallen earthly reality. Yet that kingdom and throne are indeed the very essence of reality.

Things on this earth are *not* out of control. The devil has not won and evil has not triumphed! Man is not a victim of cruel chance. We are not living on a large ball that is about to explode and send us all into oblivion. Jesus extends the invitation, "John, I want you to walk through this door and get a glimpse of Kingdom reality—a **kingdom right side up**!"

An Occupied Throne

John then writes in verse 2, "At once I was in the Spirit, and there before me was a throne in heaven with someone sitting on it." The first object glimpsed in this kingdom reality was a throne. What do you think of when you hear the word *throne*? You think of control, rule, and authority. The good news is that the powers of this world do not hold the balance of authority in this universe. I like the way John described the scene. "I saw a throne and *someone sitting on it."* (Many people in this world would have expected the throne to be unoccupied and "up for grabs." But the matter is settled in the description to follow.) It is the Sovereign God who sits on that throne. The Invisible controls and holds sway over the visible. Heaven is not only the earth's authority, but that of the whole universe as well.

An Order to Praise

Suddenly John finds himself in the middle of a mighty service of praise! He likens the appearance of God to the radiance of precious stones and sees twenty-four elders seated on lesser thrones. They are dressed in white, and crowns of gold are upon their heads. From the throne come flashes of lightning, rumblings and peals of thunder. He further sees four living creatures in the center and around the throne, one like a lion, and the others like an ox, a man, and a flying eagle. They each have six wings and are covered with eyes all around. They are speaking a continuing message: "Holy, holy, holy is the Lord God Almighty, who was, and is, and is to come." As these strange living creatures praise the God of heaven, the elders fall down in worship, and lay their crowns before the throne—saying, as they do so: "You are worthy, our Lord and God, to receive glory, and honor and power, for you created all things, and by your will they were created and have their being."

My point is this: ***the perspective of praise is none other than the throne room of the universe where we see God sitting on His throne!*** God reigns! That is the foundation of praise. When we see God as He is, we will automatically praise God as we should! Praise is a total commitment to, response to, and a confession of, the sovereign power and providence of God.

The absence of praise reveals an inadequate view of God. To know Him *is* to praise Him; and when we praise, we are aligned with heaven. Praise is being heard in heaven continuously. When we stand in the court of praise we are in the rare atmosphere of the heavenlies where God is seated on His throne in praise. As children of the Living God, we are in our element when we praise.

Amid all that bids you to run and hide and flounder in hopelessness, don't you see that same open door? Don't you hear that same thunderous voice bidding you to come? Don't you see the throne and Him who sits upon it? He is *not* wringing His hands over a world catapulting into oblivion. He does not walk around the throne with furrowed brow and worried look. He is Sovereign God! He reigns over all of Creation. Understand that, and you will be prepared to praise.

Repent of the sin of believing that things are only as they appear to be. ***Ask God to reshape your whole perspective around the vision of God on His throne.***

Our God reigns! Our God reigns! Our God reigns! Our God reigns!!

Projects in Praise

We have dealt with one theme as the basis of praise—namely the fact that our God reigns! I challenge you with two projects which will take some time but which will also yield multiple and delightful dividends.

1. Read the Psalms, marking the passages which speak of God's throne, God's reign, God's greatness, and God's authority.
2. Take a hymnal and find the songs which speak of God's greatness and sovereignty. Memorize a verse of several of these songs. (Example: "A Mighty Fortress Is Our God.")

See also Appendix A and B for additional views of praise.

A Preview of Praise

Preparing to examine the deep and delightful mysteries of praise, we stand on the mountain peak of God's sovereignty. God reigns! He is sovereign. There is a throne at the center of the universe, and upon that throne sits none other than Almighty God. From this lofty peak we can view the rich valley sprawling before us. Thus, in the first chapter we scaled the mountain. Let us now gaze upon the panorama of praise before us in the valley.

The earth was girded in praise when, for His own pleasure, God created all that is. In Job, God tolerated the incomplete information possessed by Job and his friends until, at last, He was compelled to speak:

> Who is this that darkens my counsel with words without knowledge? Brace yourself like a man; I will question you, and you shall answer me. Where were you when I laid the earth's foundations? Tell me, if you understand. Who marked off its dimensions? Surely you know! Who stretched a measuring line across it? On what were its footings set, or who laid its cornerstone … while the morning stars sang together and all the angels shouted for joy? (Job 38:2-7)

As we stand on the summit of God's sovereignty, we note that praise filled the world from the days of its beginnings. In fact, *eternity past was characterized by an atmosphere of praise.* Everything united in the chorus of praise. The stars sang together in glad anticipation of what was coming to pass. The angels shouted over the soon-to-be-revealed glory of God in His dealings with humankind.

In Revelation 4:11 the twenty-four elders, having witnessed the worship of the four living creatures, laid their crowns before the great throne of God and cried, "You are worthy, our Lord and God, to receive glory and honor and power. For you created all things, and by your will they were created and have their being." The King James Version declares, "For thy pleasure they are and were created." The whole of creation, including angels and stars, witnessed the gladness of God over the creation, and they sang and shouted in praise to God.

Praise As a Law

Praise seems to be a law written into the very structure of the universe. It seems as if everything were made to praise the Lord. Paul claims in Ephesians 1:13-14:

> And you also were included in Christ when you heard the word of truth, the of your salvation. Having believed, you were marked in him with a seal, the promised Holy Spirit, who is a deposit guaranteeing our inheritance until the redemption of those who are God's possession ... TO THE PRAISE OF HIS GLORY [caps mine].

The purpose of creation and our redemption is praise! In Isaiah 43:20*b*,21, God declared, "[These are] my chosen, the people I formed for myself THAT THEY MAY PROCLAIM MY PRAISE" (caps mine). Praise is the reason for the existence of the entire universe! It is good to note Psalm 148 here:

> Praise the Lord.
> Praise the Lord from the heavens,
> praise him in the heights above.
> Praise him, all his angels,
> praise him, all his heavenly hosts.
> Praise him, sun and moon,
> praise him, all you shining stars.
> Praise him, you highest heavens
> and you waters above the skies.
> Let them praise the name of the Lord,
> for he commanded and they were created.
> He set them in place for ever and ever;
> he gave a decree that will never pass away.
> Praise the Lord from the earth,
> you great sea creatures and all ocean depths,
> lightning and hail, snow and clouds,
> stormy winds that do his bidding,
> you mountains and all hills,
> fruit trees and all cedars,
> wild animals and all cattle,
> small creatures and flying birds,

kings of the earth and all nations,
you princes and all rulers on earth,
young men and maidens,
old men and children.
LET THEM PRAISE THE NAME OF THE LORD,
FOR HIS NAME ALONE IS EXALTED;
HIS SPLENDOR IS ABOVE THE EARTH
AND THE HEAVENS [caps mine].

Thus we see clearly that everything created in the universe has a capacity to praise the Lord. In Luke's account of the triumphal entry into Jerusalem, he reports that the "whole crowd of disciples began joyfully to praise God in loud voices for all the miracles they had seen: 'Blessed is the king who comes in the name of the Lord! Peace in heaven and glory in the highest!'" The result was that the Pharisees were tremendously incensed by this and sought Jesus to silence the praise with a stern rebuke. Jesus reproved the Pharisees, however. "'I tell you,' he replied, 'if they keep quiet, the stones will cry out.'" (Luke 19:37-40) Jesus was cognizant of the fact that if men and women—*made as the prime source of praise*—refused to do what we have been created to do, then inanimate rocks would take our place in praise.

Praise at the Close of History

Just as human history began with praise, so will praise be the background of the close of history. No book aside from the Psalms emphasizes praise more than the book of Revelation. The scene described in Revelation 4, the subject of our first chapter, was one of unprecedented praise. The praises of the four creatures sparked the praise of the elders, who left their thrones and bowed before the central throne of God. Again in Revelation 5 these same creatures and elders fell down before the throne and sang a new song focused upon the worthiness of the Lamb. Then, later in that chapter, many angels numbering "thousands upon thousands, and ten thousand times ten thousand" encircled the throne and sang, "Worthy is the Lamb, who was slain, to receive power and wealth and wisdom and strength and honor and glory and praise." After that, every creature on earth, in heaven, and in the sea joined in the mighty chorus of praise, "To him who sits on the throne and to the Lamb be praise and honor and glory and power, for ever and ever!" Throughout the Book of Revelation the elders, the four creatures, the angels, and all creation surround the events with shouts and songs of praise.

The last word in the Bible is one which is connected with praise. It is a response indicating total agreement: *Amen!* Jesus used this wonderful word as did the psalmist. It was often employed in praises in the Old Testament. "Praise be to the Lord, the God of Israel, from everlasting to everlasting. Let all the people say 'Amen!' Praise the Lord" (Psalm 106:48). In Nehemiah the people responded to the reading of the Word of God by saying, "Amen! Amen!" As David commanded the song of thanksgiving to be sung, Asaph obliged by offering the song, but all the people joined them by saying, "Amen" and "praise the Lord" (1 Chronicles 16:36). *Amen* was ranked in high company with *hallelujah* in Revelation 19:4 when the elders and the four creatures fell down and worshipped at the throne, shouting, "Amen, Hallelujah!"

Since the last word recorded in the Bible is *Amen*, it surely is appropriate for us to use it in praise and agreement with the tremendous truths of the Word concerning the greatness of our God.

Praise Is the Cloak, the Mantle of God

In Psalm 22:3 we read, "Yet you are enthroned as the Holy One; you are the praise of Israel." The King James says it more distinctly, "But thou art holy, O thou that inhabitest the praises of Israel." In other words, God lives surrounded by the praise of His creation—He "indwells" praise. Praise is His home environment.

This solves one of the vast mysteries which is connected with praise. Why is it that when we praise the Lord, things change so rapidly? Why does healing come on wings of praise? Why do human emotions undergo such transformation when praise is practiced? How are we to account for those events which accompany praise? The powerful answer is that while God is everywhere, He is not everywhere *manifested.* He is at home in praise, and there He manifests Himself best as God! When you or I choose to make God at home through praise, we invite Him to *act* at home. When God is at home, in praise, He does what it is His divine nature to do. God has an affinity for praise. He is enthroned and liberated to act mightily in praise.

Praise Is a Dividend Which God Receives as a Result of Delivering and Blessing Us

In Psalm 106:47 the psalmist requests, "Save us, O Lord our God, and gather us from the nations, *that we may give thanks to Your Holy name and glory in Your praise"* (italics mine). Thanksgiving and praise were looked upon as both the basis and the result of deliverance.

In Psalm 30:11,12 again we read, "You turned my wailing into dancing; you removed my sackcloth and clothed me with joy, *that my heart may sing to You and not be silent"* (italics mine). Again, we are delivered that we may praise Him.

In essence, then, praise is a blessing to God. One of the words for praise is *barak*, which means "to bless." It is used synonymously with praise. In 1 Chronicles 29:10, David "praised the Lord in the presence of the whole assembly." In Psalm 103, he says, "Bless the Lord, O my soul" (KJV). The *New International Version* translates the word *bless* as *praise.* God is blessed through praise. I know of no greater thought to grace the mind of man than this: *I can bless the Lord!*

Praise Is a God-given Garment to Ward Off the Spirit of Depression

The Messianic declaration of Isaiah 61:1-3 states:

> The Spirit of the Sovereign Lord is upon me, because the Lord has anointed me to preach good news to the poor. He has sent me to bind up the brokenhearted, to proclaim freedom for the captives, and release for the prisoners, to proclaim the year of the Lord's favor, and the day of vengeance of our God, to comfort all who mourn, and provide for those who grieve in Zion… to bestow on them a crown of beauty instead of ashes, the oil of gladness instead of mourning, *and a garment of praise instead of a spirit of despair* [italics mine].

No exercise or medicine will cure the ill of discouragement like praise. Depression and praise cannot live long in the same heart. They are absolutely incompatible roommates!

If I am to take this literally, I must assume that there is a spirit of despair or of depression. Many such spirits exist! Nothing terrifies the devil and his demons like praise. Praise brings the consciousness of the presence of God, with all that accompanies it. The liars from the pit cannot bring delusion in an atmosphere of praise. Since it is a garment, we can make a choice to put it on as we do a shirt, a blouse, or a coat. The constant wearing of it should then ward off any spirits of depression, discouragement, and despair.

Praise, or the Lack of It, Permits or Prohibits the Productivity of the Earth

If it is indeed a law written into the very structure of the created universe, then praise should greatly affect that created universe. God desires to bless all people but cannot do that, to His fullest desire and intention, until the people praise His name. **Praise releases God to work in His creation for maximum productivity.** This is more than implied in Psalm 67:5-7, "May the peoples praise you, O God; may all the peoples praise you. *Then the land will yield its harvest, and God, our God, will bless us. God will bless us, and all the ends of the earth will fear Him"* (caps mine).

The absence of praise permits an atmosphere in which all sorts of germs foreign to spiritual health are allowed to proliferate. Productivity is stifled. Fulfillment is limited. Man is frustrated. God is grieved. When we praise God, productivity is maximized, fulfillment is realized, and frustration is neutralized. The presence or absence of praise is pivotal in any situation. If you would enter into the theme of Psalm 47:6, "sing praises to God," you *must* praise the Lord. Productivity around you, for you, and from you will result.

Praise Glorifies God and Is the Preface to His Miraculous Deliverance

There are at least three illustrations in Scripture of the wonderful fact that praise precedes deliverance. The text supporting this claim states: "He who sacrifices thank-offerings honors me, and he prepares the way so that I may show him the salvation of God" (Psalm 50:23).

We have already referred to the first such illustration in 2 Chronicles 20. When Jehoshaphat was informed that a coalition of enemy armies was advancing toward the palace in such numbers that there was no possibility of surviving their attack, he turned to the Lord and sought His face daily. God's answer came quickly through the prophet, "Do not be afraid or discouraged because of this vast army. For the battle is not yours, but God's" (2 Chronicles 20:15*b*). The result was that they advanced toward that army with the sole weapon of praise: singing a one-line chorus, *"Give thanks to the Lord, for his love endures forever."* The Hebrew word used is *yadah*, which means to give thanks with hands extended. Thus, they went into battle. They arrived at the expected battlefront to find their nemesis, the gigantic coalition of armies, dead on the field. Praise both prepared the way and secured their deliverance.

The second illustration comes to us from Jonah 2:9. From within the belly of the whale, Jonah says, "But I, with a song of thanksgiving, will sacrifice to you. What I have vowed I will make good. Salvation comes from the Lord." At that precise point, God commanded the fish to unload its passenger immediately, and it promptly vomited Jonah onto dry land. Praise was the preface to deliverance and blessing from the Lord.

The third illustration comes from the life of Paul. Paul, Silas, and other prisoners were incarcerated in the Philippian jail. In fact, they were in stocks, a device specifically designed to be uncomfortable; yet we read in Acts 16:25 that at midnight Paul and Silas were praying and singing hymns to God. Again deliverance occurred! There was a violent earthquake, and the foundations of the prison were shaken. The doors flew open, and all the prisoners' chains fell off. Before dawn, the jailer and his family became joyful prisoners of Jesus Christ instead! Early that morning, the magistrates ordered Paul and Silas to be released and urged them to go in peace. So confident was Paul of his position and rights that he refused to be released in such a manner. He would settle for nothing less than the magistrates themselves coming to witness their release. Powerful results emerge when men sing praises and pray.

Praise Is the Chief Weapon in the Believer's Arsenal Against the Enemy

This is one of the most intriguing mysteries of praise. There are two great windows of Scripture that give us a view into this mystery. One is Psalm 8:2, "From the lips of children and infants you have ordained praise because of your enemies, to silence the foe and the avenger." The word for praise here is translated in the King James Version as "strength." When Jesus, however, quotes this passage in Matthew 21:16, He uses the word "praise."

Interestingly enough, this is not the only time praise and strength are used interchangeably. The truth is that praise is strength, and strength is praise. From the simple, the toddlers, and babes, God appoints praise because—in its essence—it stops the enemy dead in his tracks! Neither the devil nor his demons can offer any protest after praise. They are hushed. Mystery of mysteries!

Why is the devil stopped dead by praise? Why is it that the demons are so devastated by praise? I do not know the answer to these questions perfectly, but I would like to advance a theory: I believe that the devil, as Lucifer in his original state, may have been the praise leader of heaven. (See Ezekiel 28:13 in the King James Version or New King James.) Somehow, pride and egotism bested him, and he mistakenly surmised that the possibility of being greater than God was worth the risk of giving up the high privilege of praising God. So he caused a rebellion among the angels and sought to dethrone God Himself (Revelation 12).

How tragically mistaken he was; and he has lived ever since, along with his demons, in malignant regret and bitterness. The demons, in that dark world that the devil commands, followed him in that aborted rebellion and were remanded to his miserable custody. All of them, devil and demons alike, live in unrequited regret—miserable, angry, and spiteful in their plight. They find their only temporary relief by inflicting like misery on human beings.

Praise, the continuing exercise of heaven, is clearly etched into the memory of the devil and every other fallen being. The memory of the aborted revolution, in which they all lost their lofty positions, is haunting and all too clear in their consciousness. They, as few in the universe, know the power, joys, and delights of praise. When they hear Biblical praises they are driven to panic. Like fingernails on a blackboard is the sound of praises to them. They are irritated and devastated by it. I have a suspicion that they turn on each other in malignant hatred. Their ranks are broken. Their anger, hatred, and panic are heated to the boiling point. Much like jailed accomplices hate one another, the demons despise one another because of their stupidity in cooperating with the devil in bringing them to their hated end. They scream against the Praised and praisers alike, seeking by hook or crook to silence the adorations of a God they so despise. Their influence is neutralized and their lies are exposed by praise. Praise puts them to flight!

The other scripture I have in mind is Psalm 149:4-9:

> For the Lord takes delight in his people; he crowns the humble with salvation. Let the saints rejoice in this honor [praise] and sing for joy on their beds. May the praise of God be in their mouths and a double-edged sword in their hands …

(Now let me interject an explanation at this point. The mandate to praise here is not unusual. What is unusual and astounding is the manifold *purpose* of the combined praises and the word of truth. Now read the remainder of the passage.)

> … to inflict vengeance on the nations and punishment on the peoples, to bind their kings with fetters, their nobles with shackles of iron, to carry out the sentence written against them. *This is the glory of all His saints. Praise the Lord.* [italics mine].

Now read that passage again in its entirety!

Praise influences nations, kings, people, and princes. When combined with the Word of God, it speeds justice and carries out just sentences. It mediates for God in applying divinely-instituted decrees over the hordes of wickedness. Their sentences are already written and waiting to be carried out through the implementation of praise. The devil, demons, and all the evils which have resulted from their devious and destructive work have a divine sentence pronounced against them. Jesus promised that a part of the work of the Holy Spirit would be to convict the world of judgment because, said He,

"...the prince of this world now stands condemned" (John 16:11). The devil and his abominable accomplices, along with their labor and results, are sentenced by the divine court of jurisprudence. We—the saints of the Most High God—have the privilege of implementing this judgement now on earth through the means of praise. Understood? No. Believed? Yes! No wonder the psalmist in a burst of joy cried, "This is the glory of all the saints. Praise the Lord." (Psalm 149:9*b*).

These are only a few of the glorious sights visible from our lofty peak of the perspective of praise. We have viewed the valley from the mountain peak. Now we shall enter the valley to investigate the glories we have viewed from a distance.

Projects in Praise

1. Reread the stories illustrating praise as a preface to God's miraculous deliverance. Our next chapter will take note of the steps to victory through praise (2 Chronicles 20:1-30). Read all of Jonah to see how this fits into the story (Jonah 2:9). List some results credited to the praises given by Paul and Silas in the Philippian jail. (Acts 16:23-40)
2. Memorize Psalm 8:2, Psalm 50:23, and Psalm 100:4. Seek to implement them in your life this week. (Suggestion: As you approach your quiet time each day, quote Psalm 100:4 several times and break into a time of thanksgiving and praise).

The Processes of Praise

Nowhere are the procedures on praise any clearer than in the story I have referred to in 2 Chronicles 20. I suggest that you take time right now to reread that story.

So vital is our Scripture text in 2 Chronicles 20 that I have already mentioned it more than once and will likely mention it again. It provides a living lesson on both the power of perpetual praise and also the sacrifice of praise—offered when the visible realm reveals only danger and destruction. The background is a crisis of such proportion that there is absolutely no *human* alternative to despair and defeat. Jesus both warned and encouraged us in John 16:33: "In this world you will have trouble. But take heart! I have overcome the world."

Getting Acquainted with Jehoshaphat

The principal in this episode deserves our close observation. Jehoshaphat was king of Judah, the tribe whose name meant "praise the Lord." The Lord was with Jehoshaphat because in his early years he walked in the ways of David. He refused to consult with the followers of Baal, and thus the Lord established the kingdom under his control. Jehoshaphat sent teachers throughout the kingdom to instruct the people concerning the Book of the Law. Such was the blessing of God upon his reign that neighboring kingdoms dared not attack but instead brought tribute to Judah and Jehoshaphat. At the peak of his greatness, enjoying wealth and honor among the nations, Jehoshaphat allied himself with the wicked King Ahab by marriage. That mistaken alliance subjected him to the crisis conditions related in our text.

Ahab was king of Israel. He immediately asked Jehoshaphat to join him in attacking Ramoth Gilead. Both the prophets of Israel and the priests of Baal agreed that the battle should be fought, prophesying total victory. Zedekiah, son of Kenaanah, joined in their ill-fated prophecies. Only the faithful prophet Micaiah predicted that the battle would go against them. His punishment for telling the truth was a prison cell with bread and water as his fare.

Ahab never returned from that battle; he was the victim of a nameless archer. Jehoshaphat was spared because he entered the battle in disguise and was not recognized. Upon Jehoshaphat's return to his palace, he was reprimanded by Jehu for making a tragic mistake in helping the wicked and loving those who hated God. Jehu said, "There is, however, some good in you, for you have rid the land of the Asherah poles and have set your heart on seeking God" (2 Chronicles 19:3). With a severe lesson learned, Jehoshaphat seemed to turn to God more devotedly than ever before. He appointed judges in the land and demanded that they administer justice in the name of the Lord. He reminded them, "Now let the fear of the Lord be upon you. Judge carefully, for with the Lord our God there is no injustice or partiality or bribery" (2 Chronicles 19:7). In the capital city Jerusalem, he appointed priests and ordered them to administer the Law of the Lord in settling all disputes. He reminded them that if they sinned against the Lord, wrath would come upon them. His spiritual recovery from the alliance with Ahab seemed to be complete; exhorting others, Jehoshaphat said, "Act with courage, and may the Lord be with those who do well" (2 Chronicles 19:11*b*).

At this time, the peace of the palace was broken by startling news. A vast army was headed for the capital and was already in Hazazon Tamar (En Gedi). Immediately Jehoshaphat called all the people of Judah together. As they gathered, the first word from Jehoshaphat was not directed to the people, but to God (2 Chronicles 20:6-12).

A Prayer of Perspective

Backing up a little, our purpose in this chapter is observing the processes of praise, and this prayer is all-important in that observation. We see first a reminder of God's exalted position. "O Lord, God of our fathers, are you not the God who is in heaven? You rule over all the kingdoms of the nations. Power and might are in your hand, and no one can withstand you" (2 Chronicles 20:6). Now, this is a word of praise, pure and simple. Such language stills the turbulence of troubled hearts and causes faith to rise.

Then there was a recounting of God's efficient performance in the past. "O our God, did you not drive out the inhabitants of this land before your people Israel and give it forever to the descendants of Abraham your friend?" (v. 7). God had a perfect record in the past; in his prayer Jehoshaphat indicated he believed that the record would stand.

Finally, there was a stated reliance upon God's enabling power. "If calamity comes upon us, whether the sword of judgment, or plague or famine, we will stand in your presence before this temple which bears your name and will cry out to you in our distress, and you will hear and save us" (v. 9).

Steps Through the Mess

First, Jehoshaphat faced the problem squarely. He made no attempt to gloss over the seriousness of the problem. "But now here are men from Ammon, Moab, and Mount Seir, whose territory you would not allow Israel to invade when they came from Egypt; so they turned away from them and did not destroy them. See how they are repaying us by coming to drive us out of the possession you gave us as an inheritance" (vv. 10-11). The problem was serious. That fact was plain to see. It would have been a vain deception to downplay the severity of the situation.

How do we apply this for ourselves? When we're in a mess, reality therapy demands that we state our problems to God. *We* need to hear how serious the situation is. Our tendency is to play games, covering up the fact of a crisis. We often attempt to succeed at some lesser point in order to distract from the crisis at hand. Instead, we shouldn't cloud the issue with denial, blame-casting, or self-pity. We must state the problem as accurately as possible, sparing no detail for the sake of feelings. We, like Jehoshaphat, will be ready for the next significant step.

Second, Jehoshaphat ceased all trust in the flesh. This is so vital I could not possibly overstate it. Listen to Jehoshaphat's words: "...For we have no power to face this vast army that is attacking us. We do not know what to do..." (v. 12). There was a confession of human inability.

The flesh often prevents us from looking to God as our sole resource. We have been taught by our theatrical heroes and heroines that mature men and women should never admit weakness. Hogwash! The child who assumes this philosophy will never have a meaningful relationship with parents, and the believer who embraces this approach can never have an intimate relationship with God! Praise is a deathblow to the self-centeredness of the flesh. It is a denial of self-trust, self-pride, and independence. Each of us should memorize Jehoshaphat's prayer in its entirety, placing emphasis on the lines, "...we have no power … we do not know what to do..."

Third, Jehoshaphat completely concentrated on God. It is not only important to cease all trust in the powers of the flesh; it is absolutely vital to make the next right move. The last words of the prayer of Jehoshaphat were, "...but our eyes are upon you." This is the mood of all genuine praise—concentration on God. With Jehoshapat's frank admission of human infirmity and ignorance, the orientation moved solely to God. The severity of their problem was clear; the frailty of their humanity was fact. But now all eyes were upon God.

The implications of such a focus are manifold and significant. It discounts all other sources of hope and singles out God alone. It fastens our gaze upon God and determines to wait upon Him. The next action or word will come from God under such waiting.

If we look at our problems or our own weaknesses we shall soon despair. Not so with preoccupation with God. This is the heart of praise—our eyes are on You, our GOD! Praise is not problem-centered. Neither is praise human-centered. Praise is God-centered!

Fourth, they continued before God. "All the men of Judah, with their wives and children and little ones, stood there before the Lord" (2 Chronicles 20:13). This is always a necessary part of the process which brings us through to victory. It seems to be the least tolerable on our part.

There is something in all of us which finds waiting very difficult, but waiting is also a part of the mood of praise. While we wait, we are praising God. This standing before God is always a time of meditation, a time of investigation, a time of cleansing, and a time of consecration. How long are we to continue before God? Until … that's it—**until!** We are neither to light our own fire nor to manipulate the effects of our own causes. We are to wait on God, concentrating fully on Him. Time is never wasted in this effort.

Fifth, Jehoshaphat confessed the truth of God. Between the fourth and fifth steps, a very vital occurrence took place. The prophets heard from God. Such a position as that taken by Jehoshaphat generally brings a word from God. "Do not be afraid or discouraged because of this vast army. For the battle is not yours, but God's" (2 Chronicles 20:15*b*). God then proceeded to tell them exactly where the enemy would be as they advanced. The men of Judah were not to fight but only to assume their positions, stand firm, and see the salvation of the Lord God. The response of Jehoshaphat and the people was to fall down in worship while the priests stood up and praised the Lord with very loud voice (2 Chronicles 20:18,19). Jehoshaphat then made an important confession before the Lord and the people: "Listen to me, Judah and people of Jerusalem! Have faith in the Lord your God and you will be upheld; have faith in his prophets and you will be successful" (2 Chronicles 20:20*b*). There was a full agreement on the part of the people and the leadership with what they had heard from God. Their praises were a loud *Amen* to the words of God.

To hear the word of the Lord is one matter; to heed it and do it is quite another. There is a remarkable passage of Scripture in Hebrews 13:5-6, "Keep your lives free from the love of money and be content with what you have, because God has said, 'Never will I leave you; never will I forsake you.' So we say with confidence, 'The Lord is my helper; I will not be afraid. What can man do to me?'" Anything that God has said, we may boldly receive and repeat. In this case God had said the equivalent of, "This is my battle. Don't be afraid. Take your position and watch me win the war!" Their rejoicing was a sign of affirmation that the word of God was surely true.

Sixth, there was a commitment to obey. God had said, "Go out to face them tomorrow and the Lord will be with you" (2 Chronicles 20:17*b*). Early the next morning the people of Judah left for the desert of Tekoa. At this time Jehoshaphat consulted the people and appointed men to sing to the Lord on the journey. They went out at the head of the army, singing a one-line chorus: "Give thanks [praise] to the Lord, for his love endures forever!" Over and over they sang that line. The remarkably significant fact about that is that at the same time they began to sing and praise the Lord, "...the Lord set ambushes against the men of Ammon and Moab and Mount Seir who were invading Judah, and they were defeated" (2 Chronicles 20:22).

Jehoshaphat and the people of Judah had not even reached the battlefront, but their praises had released God to act—and with a deliberate suddenness, God acted! The result was that the men from Ammon and Moab turned on the men from Mount Seir, totally annihilating them. Then, without explanation, the Ammonites and the Moabites turned upon each other. No other battle recorded in military history even compares with this one.

When the men of Judah came to the place which overlooks the desert and gazed toward the vast army, all the enemy soldiers were dead. No one had escaped.

Seventh, they collected the riches from the crisis. In fact, so great was the plunder from the battle which the Lord had fought—the clothing, the equipment, the valuables—that it took three days to collect. God had turned what might have been Judah's destruction into a celebration of a glorious victory. This is the prize of praise. Praise does more than enable us to survive. It enables us to *thrive.*

On the fourth day, after the three-day period of collecting the spoils of war, they gathered in the Valley of Beracah ("Blessing Valley") where they praised the Lord. The valley gained its name from this very event. Jehosaphat and the men of Judah then returned to Jerusalem and immediately entered the Temple with harps, lutes, and trumpets. The Bible thoughtfully reports at this point, "And the kingdom of Jehoshaphat was at peace, for his God had given him rest on every side" (2 Chronicles 20:30).

Thus, we have seven steps through crisis. These steps worked for Jehoshaphat and they will work for you. Praise was the key! Notice that praise was the *preface* to the process;

praises *pervaded* the process; and praises formed the *postscript* to the process.

Projects in Praise

1. Read slowly the entire story of our Bible text (2 Chronicles 20), taking note of the pertinent points which have formed the steps I mentioned.
2. Rehearse those steps in the framework of your particular problem or need.
   A. Begin at the point of the problem. Identify it. Clarify it. Face it squarely. Be thoroughly honest about it.
   B. Cease all trust in the flesh. Admit your impotence as well as your ignorance.
   C. Concentrate on God. Say aloud, "God, I have no power against this problem, and I don't know what to do, but my eyes are on You."
   D. Continue before God **until** .... Stay in His presence, waiting until God either acts or speaks.
   E. Confess what you hear to be the truth with praise. "God has said ... therefore, I may boldly say..." Commit to obey God. If He says go, then go!
   G. Collect the riches. In God's time praise will always land you in Blessing Valley!
3. Memorize all of Jehoshaphat's prayer in 2 Chronicles 20:6-12. This will require some time, but you will find it helpful more often than you can imagine at this point.
4. Set to a tune of your own the one-line chorus that was sung by the people of Judah: "Praise the Lord, for his mercy endureth for ever." (KJV)

The Piracy of Praise

This is a good moment for us to consider one of the sternest warnings of past history. The most obvious lesson is predicated on the fact that, to a large degree, the church has suffered a theft of one of its most valuable treasures: namely praise. At some time in its not-too-distant past, the church was victimized. The result is that praise is no longer central to life. If this were no more serious than the loss of a precious commodity, that would be one thing. In the wake of its loss, however, there has come an atmosphere so foreign to praise that it produces both a fear of Biblical praise and resistance to it.

A. W. Tozer indicated this profound loss when he entitled his little book *Worship—The Missing Jewel of the Church.* The old ship, the church, has been the victim of piracy on the high seas of time. The devil has robbed us of our crown jewels: praise.

Out of the past comes a parable of this theft. In the early part of his reign, Solomon gave God the glory and remained wise and good. As a symbol of his kingdom's wealth, gold flowed like water. In 1 Kings 10:14-15 we are informed that Solomon, at the peak of his splendor, received about twenty-three metric tons of gold in revenue each year. This did not include revenues from Arabian merchants, traders, kings, and governors of the land. God had been true to His promise and had made Solomon wealthier than any king in history. No other king reigned with such wisdom, glory, splendor, and power.

Recorded in 1 Kings 10:16-17 is the story of Solomon making five hundred shields of hammered gold: two hundred large and three hundred small. They are described so we may know that the large ones contained about seven and one-half pounds of gold and the smaller ones about three and one-half pounds. The magnitude of this endeavor, as far as the value involved, initially may not be comprehended. Figuring that the large shields contained seven and one-half pounds of gold (or 112 ounces), today these shields would be worth no less than $50,000 per shield; the two hundred larger shields would be worth a total of ten million dollars; the smaller ones would be worth $25,000 each, for a total of seven and one-half million dollars! Combined, the current value of the shields would be in excess of $17,000,000.00! The dollar value of these shields, however, does not present the whole story.

The shields symbolized splendor and blessing. They were used, in all probability, at formal gatherings, on festive days, and to honor the king with his frequent royal guests. It would be challenging to imagine the splendor of Solomon's kingdom on display. His Temple was a wonder among the wonders of the world. It has been estimated that his Temple today, if duplicated with all the precious metals and stones, would cost as much as $200 billion! After the Queen of Sheba's visit to Solomon's kingdom, she marveled:

> The report I heard in my own country about your achievements and your wisdom is true. But I did not believe these things until I came and saw with my own eyes. Indeed, not even half was told me; in wisdom and wealth you have far exceeded the report I heard. How happy your men must be! How happy your officials, who continually stand before you and hear your wisdom! Praise be to the Lord your God, who has delighted in you and placed you on the throne of Israel. Because of the Lord's eternal love for Israel, he has made you king, to maintain justice and righteousness (1 Kings 10:6-9).

She responded to her impressions with gifts of gold in excess of $15 million (in today's values), and countless spices and precious stones.

History records that Solomon was blessed with greater riches and wisdom than all the other kings of the earth. The whole world sought audiences with him to hear the wisdom God had put in his heart. As the people came they brought silver, gold, spices, robes, weapons, horses, and mules. Yet, in the latter portion of his reign, the heart of Solomon became spiritually dull. He loved foreign women, and to accommodate them, he built places where temples to their detestable gods could be constructed; although God had specifically commanded him not to follow other gods. When Solomon continued to be reckless, rebellious, and headstrong, God told Solomon that He would tear the kingdom from him. Because of his father David, God would not remove the kingdom during Solomon's lifetime but would do so during the reign of his son. The kingdom began to weaken, and the nations surrounding Israel became bold, seeing Solomon's decline. So God raised up adversaries against Solomon to carry out the just punishments for his rebellion and backsliding. Jeroboam, one of his own officials, rebelled against the king. Solomon tried to kill him, but Jeroboam escaped to Egypt until Solomon's death.

Rehoboam, the son of Solomon, succeeded him as king. Headstrong like his father, he sought to institute more severe control over the people. The result was that Israel rebelled, and the kingdom was divided. Ten tribes followed Jeroboam, and two tribes—Judah and Benjamin—followed Rehoboam. Since Rehoboam was the son of Solomon by an Ammonite named Naamah, he was himself a product of Solomon's rebellion, and this rebellion continued under Rehoboam. The people continued to build sacred places for foreign gods and to engage in detestable practices carried on by their enemies, even having male prostitutes in the land.

Thus, the weakened kingdom fell prey to nations around it. The account in 1 Kings 14:25-26 reveals that King Shishak of Egypt carried off the treasures of the Temple of the Lord and of the palace. Included in this plunder were all the golden shields which Solomon had made. King Rehoboam seems to have been helpless to fend off the attack or to mount a counter-attack. Instead, he made brass shields to replace the golden ones and gave them to the commanders of the guard on duty at the entrance of the royal palace. Shields of brass for shields of gold! Tragically, this was the last recorded event in the pitiful reign of Rehoboam.

Pardon the Parable

In many important respects, the story of the stolen shields parallels the loss of praise from the church. We have noted that the enemy has robbed us of praise. How could this happen? Let's examine this metaphor piece by piece.

The Likeness of Gold to Praise

Gold and praise are similar in many important respects. Gold has been the standard of value in virtually every society. Similarly, the nature of praise is that it draws attention continually to high standards. As gold is recognized universally, *hallelujah*—the premier word for praise—is pronounced the same in every major language on earth!

Gold is difficult to destroy; in fact, even when heated to boiling, gold is not injured. The result is actually that a finer quality of metal is produced. Likewise, our praise becomes more refined when impure motives are driven out in the heat of tribulation. Because of its physical attributes, gold has served as a symbol of excellence, purity, and blessing. Praise focuses on the same.

The Bible pictures gold as being so plentiful in heaven that even the streets are paved with this pure material. It is not going to be more plentiful than praise, however; in heaven, praise to our God will continually fill our mouths and our ears.

Can anything else be used as a substitute for gold or for praise? We shall see.

The Symbolism of the Shields

A shield provides protection in battle. (We have seen how praise can accomplish this as well.) Solomon's golden shields, however, were designed not for warfare but for testimony. They were a sign of God's blessings upon the nation, and their excellence served as a motivation to the people. When the shields were lined up for hundreds of yards, the gleaming rays of the sun blazing on the shields spoke volumes to visiting dignitaries, as well as to the populace of Israel. All witnessed the blessings of God upon Solomon and his kingdom.

The Stolen Shields

When Shishak took the treasures of the kingdom, including the golden shields, the theft was an indication of consummate weakness on the part of Israel. Their national heart was gone; they had no power either to resist the enemy or to recover the plunder taken in the attack. Splendor, glory, and blessing had departed from the nation.

In the same way, our spiritual defenses have weakened over

the years as we focused on man-made traditions (our own glory), and the enemy has stolen Biblical praise from our midst. As it is with our churches, so it is with our nation and with individuals as well. The splendor, glory, and blessing have departed as we have made ourselves vulnerable to attack.

The Substitute Shields

Almost as pathetic as the loss of the golden shields was the response of Rehoboam. Brass being plentiful and cheap, and from a distance appearing like gold, Rehoboam had new shields made of brass. This compromise with quality cost him very little. The shields would shine if enough human elbow grease (a work of the flesh) were applied. People who were uncaring or undiscerning might not realize for a time that a substitution had been made, although eventually the brass would tarnish unmistakably.

Haven't we made similar substitutions? As we study Biblical praise, we will understand more clearly how poor a bargain is made in substituting the brass of form and order for the gold of spontaneous worship and adoration. In promoting our own dignity and pride, we have produced something which no longer looks like the real thing even at a distance, so tarnished and impure has our praise become.

Formerly the golden shields lined the path to the house of the Lord, welcoming and revealing the king in all his regal splendor. True praise will do the same, welcoming God in His splendor and revealing His glory.

The Value of Praise

Gold does not depreciate, nor does praise! For the church, praise is not only the symbol of excellence and blessing, it is our chief means of protection and our primary weapon. We must risk ridicule and opposition and personally repent in order to recover praise. We must not settle for anything less than true Biblical praise. Its loss has been costlier than we can imagine, but its recovery will solve a multitude of ills.

The enemy recognizes the value of praise as well, and he will do all he can to keep the Church content with weak substitutions. Compromise, the primary sin, has been followed by our capitulation to peer-group opinion and public sentiment.

A Word to the Church

Thomas McCauley, a British historian who died on the eve of the Civil War in America, wrote a warning to America: "Your republic will be laid waste by barbarians in the twentieth century as Rome was in the fifth century with this difference ... the Huns and vandals who ravaged the empire came from without while your Huns and vandals will attack from within ... engendered by your own institutions."

This was rare wisdom, written more than 135 years ago! Let the church, the nation, and individual believers return to praise, to genuine Biblical worship. May we repent of the tendency toward tameness and passivity and refuse the relentless pressure to stay with the pack, to conform to the crowd, and to identify with the status quo. We need to know that life is a battle won by decisions, decisions made in a moment but lived out in subsequent years. Let us choose excellence, value, glory! Away with the brass shields of costless compromise! Like David when he was offered the threshing floor as a gift, let us say, "I will not sacrifice to the Lord with that which cost me nothing!"

May the tragic story of Rehoboam and his shields of mere brass serve as a means of conviction, as well as a motivation for recovering the gold of true worship in our lives, individually and corporately.

Projects in Praise

1. Read background material on the kingdom of Solomon to review the place of praise in his life and that of the nation. Scriptures which deserve special note are 1 Kings 3:1-15 and 1 Kings 8-9. (These chapters give an idea of the greatness of the kingdom and the centrality of praise).
2. List the commandments of God broken by Solomon toward the end of his reign; e.g. taking foreign wives, tolerating foreign gods, and the like.
3. Meditate on losses suffered by yourself or the Church through compromises today. Watch out for substitute shields!

5 The Person We Praise

"From the rising of the sun to the place where it sets, the name of the Lord is to be praised."
(Psalm 113:3)

Over and over again we are exhorted to praise the name of the Lord. The third commandment states, "Thou shalt not take the name of the Lord thy God in vain" (Exodus 20:7). Why are we commanded to praise the *name* of the Lord? The answer to this question is of tremendous significance to our study of praise. Let us review some of the Scriptures which speak of His name.

> O Lord, our Lord, how majestic is your name in all the earth (Psalm 8:1).
> Ascribe to the Lord the glory due his name (Psalm 29:2).
> Sing to the Lord, you saints of his; praise his holy name (Psalm 30:4).
> Glorify the Lord with me; let us exalt his name together (Psalm 34:4).
> Like your name, O God, your praise reaches to the ends of the earth (Psalm 48:10).
> They sing praise to your name (Psalm 66:4).
> Praise be to his glorious name forever... (Psalm 72:19)
> Give thanks to him and praise his name (Psalm 100:4*b*).
> Every day I will praise you and extol your name for ever and ever (Psalm 145:2).

Why do we praise the *name* of the Lord? In Oriental thought, as contrasted with western practice, a name is never used merely to keep from confusing that person with someone else. The name was used as an expression of the *kind* of person they were or would become. Thus, the name (or names) for God stand for His manifold nature. His names are simply descriptions of Himself and of His activities. The names for God are, in a real sense, one of His means of self-revelation. These names are not human inventions but divine, though they are borrowed from human language and human relationships. God is incomprehensible, but in His names He condescends to all that is finite and becomes like a man. On the one hand, we cannot know Him because He is unknowable. On the other hand, we can know Him because He has given us His names. These names are given to us that we might have a *measure* of revelation about Him and come to know Him. They are designations of God, not of His deepest essence, but what we can know of Him as He relates Himself to us in His redemptive activities.

Since we are engaged in a study of praise, it only seems fitting that we should investigate the names of the One we are called upon to praise. In this chapter we will look at what are commonly referred to as the redemptive names of God, so called because they convey to us how God relates to us within the framework of redemption. But let us first look at some of the common names for God employed in the Old Testament.

Elohim

Elohim is the name of God we meet in the first chapter of Genesis, and it is used over 2,700 times in the Bible. It occurs in the first chapter of Genesis thirty-two times. The derivation of this name is generally accepted to be from *El*, signifying the "one who is great, mighty, dreadful." It is the *Elohim* who creates, by His spoken word, all that is. (Genesis 1:1) He says and it is done. He brings into being that which was not.

Some say that *Elohim* is derived from the word *alah* which is said to mean "to declare or to swear." There is no conflict here either way, for the greatness of God guarantees God the absolute right to initiate covenants and to name the terms. Also, the name *Elohim* is a plural name for God. The first obvious implication of this is that it suggests the Trinity. Beyond this implication is the intensive use of the plural to denote completeness.

El Shaddai

We have already viewed the meaning of *El* as "great and glorious." *Shaddai* occurs forty-eight times in the Old Testament and always is translated "Almighty." The prime suspect as a derivative is a word meaning "breast," implying nourishment, satisfaction, and supply. Putting the two parts of this name together we have *El Shaddai*, "the one who is mighty to completely nourish, satisfy, and supply us." In the Septuagint, the name *Shaddai* is rendered a number of times by the Greek word *Hikanos*, which can be translated "all-sufficient." It is the name under which God made great and mighty promises to Abraham and Jacob (Genesis 35:11). As God initiated the covenant with Abraham in Genesis 17:1, He said, "I am *El Shaddai*" [God Almighty].

Adonai

As a name for God this name occurs some 300 times in the Old Testament. When referring to God, this name is almost always in the plural, and refers to God's ownership and rulership of everything that is. If we understood this name alone, it would change our lives! *Adonai* suggests Lordship on His part, and stewardship and submission on our part. It is this name that Isaiah used when he described the scene in Isaiah 6, "In the year that King Uzziah died, I saw the Lord [*Adonai*] seated on a throne, high and exalted..." Isaiah's earthly lord had died, but his heavenly Lord was sitting on a throne—very much alive, in control, and worthy to be praised!

The name *Adonai,* in the Greek Old Testament, is *Kurios* or "Lord." It is used in connection with the name *YHWH,* or, as it has been translated more recently, *Jehovah,* some 200 times in the Book of Ezekiel alone. The significance of this usage is that *Jehovah*, the One Who Is, claims to be at the same time the One Who reigns.

Thus, when we are called upon to praise the name of God, all of these implications are involved and more.

Jehovah

The word Jehovah comes from *YHWH,* the most commonly used designation for God in the Bible. It is used more than 6,800 times! It is derived from the verb translated "to be." Moses Maimonides, the most-noted Jewish commentator of the Middle Ages, wrote of this name for God, "All the names for God that occur in the Scriptures are derived from His works except one, and that is Jehovah; and this is called the plain name because it teaches plain and unequivocally of the substance of God." In Exodus 3:14, in answer to Moses' question as to God's identity, God declared, "I AM WHO I AM. This is what you are to say to the Israelites: 'I AM has sent me to you.'" That is the essence of the name Jehovah.[1] He is the ever-living One, the only-living One, the self-existent One, and is dependent on no one or nothing outside Himself. He is self-existent and self-sufficient.

These "common names"bring us to the heart of our study of the redemptive names for God. All of the following names are connected with the name Jehovah and are also referred to as the *compound* names for God. I also love to call them the *covenant* names for God, because they relate to us how the Covenant God deals with His covenant children. Remember, we are studying them in the light of their significance to praise.

Jehovah-Jireh

We find this name for God in Genesis 22:14. The word for *Jireh* is one which means "to see." The setting is on Mount Moriah. God has commanded Abraham to sacrifice Isaac, his only son, on the altar. Our imaginations run wild when we try to describe the scene.

God gives the order and Abraham, realizing the nature of his covenant relationship with El Shaddai, asks no questions and proceeds to obey. They come to the foot of the mount and leave the servants with the promise that they will return again.

On the way up the mountain, the beloved son of promise—

---

1. Note: Herbert Wolf in his scholarly book *An Introduction to the Old Testament Pentateuch* enlightens us further:

The personal name for God, whose meaning was explained most fully to Moses, was "Yahweh," better known as "Jehovah." The exact pronunciation of this name is not clear; only the four consonants–YHWH–are given in the Hebrew Bible. In scholarly discussion the intriguing name is sometimes called the tetragrammaton, the Greek word for "four letters." The vowels are not indicated because the Jews eventually refused to pronounce the name, not wanting to take the name of Yahweh in vain (Ex. 20:7) and perhaps to prevent pagan people from misusing it. When this sacred name appeared in a verse the Jews pronounced it "Adonay," the other word for "Lord" (see below). The vowels of "Adonay" were merged with YHWH to produce "Yehowah" (=Jehovah). The correct pronunciation was probably closer to "Yahweh,," whose first syllable is preserved in "Hallelujah"–that is, "Praise Yah"–"Yah" being a shortened form of "Yahweh." Most modern translations avoid the problem by using "Lord" to render this name.

When Moses asked God what name he should use when the Israelites inquired as to who sent him to lead the nation from Egypt, God said to tell them that "I AM has sent me to you" (Ex. 3:14). Since "I AM" is a word spelled almost like "YHWH," we are quite sure that it holds the key to the meaning of this most intimate name for God. In verse 12 God says, "I will be with you," and this is likely the way "I AM" is also to be understood.

the son of Abraham's old age—asks the question, "Here is the fire and here is the wood, but where is the sacrifice?"Out of the breaking heart of Abraham comes the soft reply, "Son, God will provide." On top of the mountain they construct a crude altar and prepare it for use. Abraham sadly divulges that his son Isaac is the sacrifice. Obedient Isaac is laid upon the altar, and Abraham raises his knife to take Isaac's life with one swift movement. At that exact instant a voice from heaven, an angel, calls to him, "Abraham, do not touch the child. Now I know that you fear God, because you have not withheld from me your son, your only son."

He then shows him a ram caught in a nearby thicket. Abraham unbinds Isaac with delight and sacrifices the ram instead, crying out, "We will call the name of this place **Jehovah-Jireh**."

Thus, the name *Jehovah-Jireh* means "the Lord provides." Now that is mystifying until we look more deeply into the meaning. The word "provide" is taken from two Latin words—*pro* meaning "first" or "before" and *vide* meaning "to see." The two words together obviously mean "to see before." So, we have in this compound name for God one who "sees to everything beforehand." God has, in fact, stood at the beginning of history and has seen to the very end of history, and beyond; and He has seen to everything. Any need we will ever have is already met in Him. Praise *Jehovah-Jireh!*

Jehovah-Rophe

This name is in Exodus 15:26. The word *rophe* always means to heal, restore, or cure. Unlike the name *Jehovah-Jireh* which was given by Abraham, this one, *Jehovah-Rophe*, was given by God of Himself. The scene is at Elim after the crisis at the bitter waters of Marah. God makes a promise to them: "If you listen carefully to the voice of the Lord your God and do what is right in his eyes, if you pay attention to all his commands and keep all his decrees, I will not bring on you any of the diseases I brought on the Egyptians, for I am the Lord who heals you [*Jehovah Rophe*]." God did not only promise to heal. He did better than that. He said, "Healing is what I am!" Praise *Jehovah-Rophe*!

Jehovah-Nissi

This name confronts us in Exodus 17:15. *Nissi* means "a standard" or "a banner."Amalek had stood in the path of God's people and contested their right to go on. There Moses told Joshua to go down into the valley and fight Amalek. Meanwhile, Moses would stand on the mountain with the rod of God in his hand. The historical connection is that groups of people in those days had banners around which they gathered as a means of identity. It was not always a flag but was sometimes only a pole or rod which was visible to all the group. That rod represented the power of God upon a human life. After learning the lesson of the relationship between the rod on the mount and the battle in the valley, the conflict was settled with victory belonging to the Israelites. In the Valley of Rephidim, Moses recognized that God was the standard to which all Israel must continually gather. Thus, he celebrated by building a memorial to God in the valley, calling it *Jehovah-Nissi.* The derivation is from a word meaning "to glisten." Jews often used the same word for "miracle." What was Moses saying in referring to God as *Jehovah-Nissi?* He was saying, "God is our banner of identity, our flag of victory, our shining pole of gathering." When the battle rages fiercely we are to stay with the "standard"—*Jehovah-Nissi!* Praise *Jehovah-Nissi.*

Jehovah-M'Kaddesh

This name is found in Leviticus 20:8. It means "to set apart for divine use" and follows the command on God's part for our holiness. How sweet this name sounds to our ears as we realize that holiness is a quality we, in our mere humanity, cannot attain. How reassuring when God says, "I am the Lord, who makes you holy [*Jehovah-M'Kaddesh*]!" This term for sanctification is used some 700 times in the Old Testament. The word was used for articles consecrated for the worship of Jehovah. Now *we* are the temples of God, and God lives in us through the Holy Spirit! He is the One who makes us holy. Praise *Jehovah-M'Kaddesh*!

Jehovah-Shalom

In Judges 6:24 Gideon builds an altar, calling it *Jehovah-Shalom.* The word *shalom* means "peace" but is also translated "full, complete, finished, or perfected." The story in Judges illustrates the value of peace by way of contrast:

Because God's people did that which was evil in His sight, He turned them over to the Midianites for discipline. They had no peace. When they planted their crops, the enemy would invade the country and ruin them. The people of God were impoverished by this continual raiding and they called upon God. Gideon was threshing some wheat, hiding in his winepress under an oak in Ophrah, when an angel of the Lord came to him with the surprising greeting, "The Lord is with you, mighty warrior."

This so amazed Gideon that he replied, "If the Lord is with us, why has all this happened to us? Where are all his wonders?" The angel informed Gideon that he (Gideon) would be the means whereby his people would be delivered. Not certain of the reality of it all, Gideon requested the angel to stay there until he could go and fetch a sacrifice. The response of the angel to the sacrifice would, in Gideon's eyes, confirm his genuineness.

Gideon came back with meat and broth and put them on a rock before the angel. The angel reached out with the staff in his hand, and the sacrifice was immediately consumed by fire. At this Gideon exclaimed, "Ah, Sovereign Lord! I have seen the angel of the Lord face to face!"

Then God spoke to him in consolation, "Peace! Do not be afraid. You are not going to die!"

Gideon exclaimed aloud, "*Jehovah-Shalom*! [God is peace!]" (Judges 6:11-24).

In a time of war Gideon found that God not only gave peace, He *is* peace. This is a rest that all people need. Jehovah is our complete peace. Praise *Jehovah-Shalom!*

Jehovah-Rohi

The first statement in Psalm 23:1 is the next name for God that evokes our praise. It means "God is our Shepherd." The spirit of the name is perfectly carried out in the remainder of the Psalm.

No other name has the tender, intimate touch this one does. All that a good shepherd is to his sheep, God is to His people. His guidance is so perfect that we have no lack. We are made to lie down in green pastures. We are led by waters that are still and untroubled. Our souls are restored and we are led in righteous paths. We may walk through death's dark valley without fear. We are comforted by His rod and staff. Our enemies glare helplessly as we sit at laden tables. Our heads are anointed and our cups run over. We are flanked by goodness and mercy all the days of our lives, and the house of the Lord is our eternal home. All of this is because He is our *rohi*, our Shepherd.

Revelation 7:17 adds to this picture: "For the Lamb at the center of the throne will be their shepherd; he will lead them to springs of living water. And God will wipe away every tear from their eyes." Praise the Lamb who is our Shepherd! Praise *Jehovah-Rohi*!

Jehovah-Tsidkenu

The word *tsidek* means "to be stiff or straight." Essentially it simply means "to be right." The background behind this name is both tragic and glorious. The nation was in dire straits. Judah was hastening toward its fall; the people were oppressed; violence was everywhere. Though King Josiah had instituted reforms and revival had come, the wickedness of the people was too entrenched. Those who had been assigned the responsibility of spiritual care had scattered the flocks. The prophets had lied. But God told of a better day in Jeremiah 23:5-6:

> "The days are coming," declares the Lord, "when I will raise up to David a righteous Branch, a King who will reign wisely and do what is just and right in the land. In his days Judah will be saved and Israel will live in safety. This is the name by which he will be called: The Lord our Righteousness [*Jehovah-Tsidkenu*]."

God is the "entirely just and righteous One." Righteousness is straight and narrow. A pound is sixteen ounces, never fifteen or seventeen. A foot is twelve inches, never eleven or thirteen. God's measurements are exact. He requires righteousness. This name reveals that ***He becomes to us what He requires of us.*** In 1 Corinthians 1:30 we are informed that Christ has become our righteousness." Praise *Jehovah-Tsidkenu!*

Jehovah-Shammah

This name for God appears at the very end of the book of Ezekiel (48:35). It means "the Lord is there." Like many of the prophets' messages, Ezekiel's was sad indeed. The nation was in decline in every way. The meeting place where God met His people had been so desecrated that God took leave from His house. The nation had lost its spirit. Yet, like other prophets, Ezekiel offered hope at the end.

The presence of God means everything. The Tabernacle and Temple were where God lived among His people. We cannot understand their full significance as they suggested the very *presence* of Jehovah among His own. On the exact site of Abraham's experience in offering Isaac to the Lord, Solomon constructed the Temple. God was there with Abraham and God was there with Solomon. His glory was such that the priests ceased their functions!

Now under Ezekiel, with the glory having departed from the Temple, he shared a vision of hope with His people. The last facet of that glorious vision was about a city. That city was to be named *Jehovah-Shammah* ("The Lord is there"). A better day was coming. God was coming back to His Temple.

Where on earth does God live now? He is at home in His temples—you and me! At Pentecost the fire that had departed the Temple in Ezekiel's day returned, and mortal men and women became temples of the living God! Jehovah is there! Paul declared it in 1 Corinthians 3:16: "Don't you know that you yourselves are God's temple and that God's Spirit lives in you?" Again, as he refers to the arrangements under the new covenant in 2 Corinthians 6:16, he says, "…For we are the temple of the living God. As God has said: 'I will live with them and walk among them, and I will be their God, and they will be my people.'" *Jehovah-Shammah* is in us!

Having reviewed the eight covenant or redemptive names for our God, I want you to remember several important truths as we come to the close of this chapter:

1. God's character is revealed through His names.
2. God reveals our need through His names.
3. The nature of our redemption is revealed through His names.
4. We can know what to expect of life through His names.
5. We can come to know God better through His names.
6. We can come to know the riches of our true identity through His names.
7. Praising the names of God brings to light that particular characteristic.

We have already learned that God inhabits the praises of His people. We could even say that praise is His home address or He is at home in praise. How personal this makes the names of God! Realizing that God is all that His names suggest, we know that although He is everywhere, praise brings about the *manifestation* of God.

May I suggest an example? Here you are. The cupboard is bare. The "wolf is at the door." You are compelled by reason to give up. But just as you do, you remember that one of God's names is JEHOVAH-JIREH. Instead of giving up, you give in to your spiritual judgment and praise the name of God *Jehovah-Jireh*! He was always *Jehovah-Jireh*, but in your praises He is liberated to manifest Himself as your Provider.

You are sick in mind, emotions, spirit, and/or body. You are about to fall into deep depression. You are reminded that God has another name: JEHOVAH-ROPHE, our healer! Call Him what He is! He is what He is always. But now He is free to manifest Himself to you in what He is when you praise Him!

The battle is fierce. You are tempted to hoist the white flag. The ranks are breaking around you. The enemy is breaking through. God has a name that fits here: JEHOVAH-NISSI. He is our banner of victory. He is our sign of triumph. Thanks be to Him who always causes us to triumph!

You are disturbed. Your inner peace is broken. Your soul is in unrest. Things are going badly. God has a name for this as well: JEHOVAH-SHALOM, our peace.

Notice each of these names reveal not only what He gives but what He *is*. You may provide the examples for the remainder of the names. I dare you: Try to find a need in your life not covered by one of His names. GOD IS ALL OF THESE.

But where does Jesus come into all of this? Jesus is the full revelation of God. In Him every promise of God was "yea" and "amen." It is by His sending the Holy Spirit to dwell in us (John 15:26) that Jesus reveals the fullness of God to us and in us. We have come to God through Christ. We know Him through Christ. In Jesus' prayer in John 17, He prayed, "I have given them [us] the glory that you gave me, that they may be one as we are one." The glory of Christ was the presence of the Father in Him. Our glory is the presence of

Christ in us through the Spirit. Paul said, "To them God has chosen to make known among the Gentiles the glorious riches of this mystery, which is Christ in you, the hope of glory" (Colossians 1:27). One great and glorious fact we need to remember is this: ALL THAT GOD IS, HE IS IN HIS NAMES; AND ALL THAT HE IS IN HIS NAMES, HE WAS IN CHRIST. ALL THAT HE IS IN CHRIST, HE IS IN US! Praise Jehovah!

Projects in Praise

1. List the eight compound names in your prayer notebook for use in praise.
2. Prepare your Bible for sharing these names by chain-referencing. Example: Put in the flyleaf of your Bible the first reference to Jehovah-Jireh–Genesis 22:14. Turn in your Bible to Genesis 22:14 and write the next reference–Exodus 17:15–in the margin. Continue this until you have covered all the compound names we have listed.
3. Choose the name among the eight which best fits your greatest need right now. Speak to God, addressing Him, as "Jehovah-________." Meditate on the meaning of that name, remembering the reference where it originated. Praise God with the use of that particular name and let Him be to you what He is.
4. Use these names regularly in your quiet time and through the day. You will discover this to be a wonderful worship experience.

PRAISE JEHOVAH*

Praise the Name of Jesus, Praise the Name of Jesus,
He's my Rock, He's my Fortress,
He's my Deliverer, In Him will I trust.
Praise the Name of Jesus.

Praise Jehovah-Jireh, Praise Jehovah-Jireh,
He's my Source, He's my Sufficiency,
He's my Provider, In Him will I trust.
Praise Jehovah-Jireh.

Praise Jehovah-Rophe, Praise Jehovah-Rophe,
He's my Health, He's my Healing,
He's my Physician, In Him will I trust.
Praise Jehovah-Rophe.

Praise Jehovah-Nissi, Praise Jehovah-Nissi,
He's my Flag, He's my Banner,
He's my Victory, In Him will I trust.
Praise Jehovah-Nissi.

Praise Jehovah-M'kaddesh, Praise Jehovah-M'kaddesh,
He's my Light, He's my Holiness,
He's my Sanctity. In Him will I trust.
Praise Jehovah-M'kaddesh.

Praise Jehovah-Shalom, Praise Jehovah-Shalom,
He's my Peace, He's My Comfort,
He's My Security, In Him will I trust.
Praise Jehovah-Shalom.

Praise Jehovah-Rohi, Praise Jehovah-Rohi,
He's my Guide, He's my Shepherd,
He's my Protector, In Him will I trust.
Praise Jehovah-Rohi.

Praise Jehovah-Tsidkenu, Praise Jehovah-Tsidkenu,
He's my Life, He's my Redemption,
He's my Righteousness, In Him will I trust.
Praise Jehovah-Tsidkenu.

Praise Jehovah-Shammah, Praise Jehovah-Shammah,
He's my Friend, He's my Faithfulness,
He's Omnipresent, In Him will I trust.
Praise Jehovah-Shammah.

*This poem was composed by Doug Alexander, while a staff member of the First Baptist Church, Little Rock, Arkansas. You may sing it to the tune of the chorus, "Praise the Name of Jesus."

The Pathway to Praise

"Be joyful always; pray continually; give thanks in all circumstances, for this is God's will for you in Christ Jesus" (1 Thessalonians 5:16-18).

Having outlined much of the conceptual side of praise, we need to interject a practical discussion on how to enter into the practice of praise. One seldom moves from one place to another in one giant step. It is generally done in a series of smaller steps—likewise with praise.

Our text does not use the word *praise*, but the fact is that if one will obey the three injunctions contained in it, praise will be the result. The absence of any one of these will prohibit praise from its fullest expression; however, the presence of these three exercises in any life will land it in the center of praise.

The Choice to Rejoice

The Bible speaks much of joy. One does not have to read the Bible a great deal to be convinced that God wants His people to be joyful. God is a joyful God. Nehemiah spoke to his people and said, "Go and enjoy choice food and sweet drinks, and send some to those who have nothing prepared. This day is sacred to our Lord. Do not grieve, for *the joy of the Lord is your strength* (Nehemiah 8:10, italics mine).

The people of God, when in right standing with Him, were a joyful people. The Psalms are filled with joy.

> But let all who take refuge in you be glad; let them ever sing for joy (Psalm 5:11*a*).
>
> You have made known to me the path of life; you will fill me with joy in your presence, with eternal pleasures at your right hand (Psalm 16:11).
>
> You turned my wailing into dancing; you removed my sackcloth and clothed me with joy (Psalm 30:11).

I will be glad and rejoice in your love, for you saw my affliction and knew the anguish of my soul (Psalm 31:7).
Sing joyfully to the Lord, you righteous; it is fitting for the upright to praise him (Psalm 33:1).
Sing to him a new song; play skillfully, and shout for joy (Psalm 33:3).
But may all who seek you rejoice and be glad in you; may those who love your salvation always say, "The Lord be exalted!" (Psalm 40:16)

David remembered how he used to travel with the multitude to the house of God with "...shouts of joy and thanksgiving among the festive throng" (Psalm 42:4*b*). Three times he speaks to his disturbed soul in Psalm 42:5,11 and Psalm 43:5: "Why are you downcast, O my soul? Why so disturbed within me? Put your hope in God, for I will yet praise him, my Savior and my God."

Clap your hands, all you nations; shout to God with cries of joy (Psalm 47:1).
God has ascended amid shouts of joy, the Lord amid the sounding of trumpets (Psalm 47:5).
Shout with joy to God all the earth! (Psalm 66:1).
My lips will shout for joy when I sing praise to you—I, whom you have redeemed (Psalm 71:23).
Sing for joy to God our strength; shout aloud to the God of Jacob! (Psalm 81:1).
Blessed are those who have learned to acclaim you, who walk in the light of your presence, O Lord. They rejoice in your name all the day long; they exult in your righteousness (Psalm 89:15-16).
For you make me glad by your deeds, O Lord; I sing for joy at the work of your hands (Psalm 92:4).
Come, let us sing for joy to the Lord; let us shout aloud to the Rock of our salvation (Psalm 95:1).
Rejoice in the Lord, you who are righteous, and praise his holy name (Psalm 97:12).
Shout for joy to the Lord, all the earth, burst into jubilant song with music (Psalm 98:4).
Let the rivers clap their hands, let the mountains sing together for joy (Psalm 98:8).
May my meditation be pleasing to him, as I rejoice in the Lord (Psalm 104:34).
Let them sacrifice thank offerings and tell of his works with songs of joy (Psalm 107:22).

Shouts of joy and victory resound in the tents of the righteous (Psalm 118:15*a*).

This is the day the Lord has made; let us rejoice and be glad in it (Psalm 118:24).

The Lord has done great things for us, and we are filled with joy (Psalm 126:3).

May your priests be clothed with righteousness; may your saints sing for joy (Psalm 132:9).

Let the saints rejoice in this honor and sing for joy on their beds (Psalm 149:5).

Isaiah's message has frequent references to *joy*:

With joy you will draw water from the wells of salvation. Shout aloud and sing for joy, people of Zion, for great is the Holy One of Israel among you (Isaiah 12:3,6).

They will enter Zion with singing; everlasting joy will crown their heads. Gladness and joy will overtake them, and sorrow and sighing will flee away (Isaiah 35:10).

Let the desert and its towns raise their voices; let the settlements where Kedar lives rejoice. Let the people of Sela sing for joy; let them shout from the mountain tops (Isaiah 42:11).

Sing for joy, O heavens, for the Lord has done this; shout aloud, O earth beneath. Burst into song, you mountains, you forests and all your trees, for the Lord has redeemed Jacob, he displays his glory in Israel (Isaiah 44:23).

The ransomed of the Lord will return. They will enter Zion with singing; everlasting joy will crown their heads. Gladness and joy will overtake them, and sorrow and sighing will flee away (Isaiah 51:11).

You will go out with joy and be led forth in peace; the mountains and hills will burst into song before you, and all the trees of the field will clap their hands (Isaiah 55:12).

And to provide for those who grieve in Zion–to bestow on them a crown of beauty instead of ashes, the oil of gladness [joy] instead of mourning and a garment of praise instead of a spirit of despair (Isaiah 61:3).

I delight greatly in the Lord; my soul rejoices in my God. For he has clothed me with garments of salvation and arrayed me in a robe of righteousness (Isaiah 61:10).

As a young man marries a maiden, so will your sons marry you; as a bridegroom rejoices over his bride, so will your God rejoice over you (Isaiah 62:5).

But be glad and rejoice forever in what I will create, for I will create Jerusalem to be a delight and its people a joy. I will rejoice over Jerusalem and take delight in my people; the sound of weeping and of crying will be heard in it no more (Isaiah 65:18-19).

Rejoice with Jerusalem and be glad for her, all you who love her; rejoice greatly with her, all you who mourn over her (Isaiah 66:10).

Jeremiah is known as "the weeping prophet." Yet he is heard to say:

"When your words came, I ate them; they were my joy and my heart's delight, for I bear your name, O Lord God Almighty" (Jeremiah 15:16).

His message of judgment was tempered with joy:

From them will come songs of thanksgiving and the sound of rejoicing (Jeremiah 30:19).

This is what the Lord says: "Sing with joy for Jacob; shout for the greatest of the nations" (Jeremiah 31:7*a*).

Then maidens will dance and be glad, young men and old as well. I will turn their mourning into gladness; I will give them comfort and joy instead of sorrow (Jeremiah 31:13).

The case for joy continues as we see Jesus, our joyful Savior, bringing joy wherever He goes. (I have used italics in the following verses for emphasis.) He says in John 15:11, "I have told you this so that my *joy* may be in you and that your joy may be complete." When His coming was announced there was joy. "I bring you good news of great *joy* that will be for all the people" (Luke 2:10). Mary's song begins with a shout of joy, "...My soul praises the Lord and my spirit *rejoices* in God my Savior" (Luke 1:46-47). Jesus encouraged joy, even in the worst of circumstances. He said, "Blessed are you when men hate you, when they exclude you and insult you and reject your name as evil, because of the Son of Man. *Rejoice* in that day and leap for joy, because great is your reward in heaven..." (Luke 6:22-23). The life of Jesus was a life of incorruptible joy. The writer of Hebrews gives us insight into the deep joy of Jesus even as he went to the cross: "Let us fix our eyes on Jesus, the author and perfecter of our faith, who for the *joy* set before him endured the cross, scorning its shame, and sat down at the right hand of the throne of God" (Hebrews 12:2).

Paul was an apostle of joy. He reminds us in Romans 14:17-18, "For the kingdom of God is not a matter of eating and drinking, but of righteousness, peace, and *joy* in the Holy Spirit, because anyone who serves Christ in this way is pleasing to God and approved by men." He assured us that a facet of the fruit of the Spirit was joy (Galatians 5:22). He wrote his most joyful epistle from a prison cell. In the midst of it he commanded, "Finally, my brothers, rejoice in the Lord! … Rejoice in the Lord always. I will say it again: Rejoice!" (Philippians 3:1,4:4). Even in the face of all his trials he anticipated the finishing of his course with joy (Acts 20:24).

The heritage we have received from the church of the New Testament is one of gladness and celebration. "They broke bread in their homes and ate together with glad and sincere hearts, praising God and enjoying the favor of all the people" (Acts 2:46*b*-47*a*).

I have gone to minute detail in putting across what may be one of the most important points to understand. Joy is necessary to praise. I am not speaking of light and fluffy feelings of emotion or of shallow silliness. I am speaking of genuine joy in the Lord. Obviously joy is not the consensus of emotions but a spiritual choice. No wonder that George Mueller said, "The first thing to be concerned about was not how much I might serve the Lord, or how I might glorify the Lord, but how I might get my soul in a happy state, and how my inner man might be nourished."

Therefore, our first responsibility as we prepare for praise is to make the choice to practice joy!

The Persistence to Pray

We are not only to make the choice to rejoice, we are to be persistent in prayer. Though it is a physical impossibility to pray all the time, it is a joyful possibility that we may be in a prayerful spirit all the time. It is a matter of developing the Godward look. The regular time that we spend with God is absolutely necessary and will render us more likely to remain in a frame of prayerfulness.

Jabez is a clear example of one who prayed persistently. He stood out among his peers and, though his name literally means *pain*, he developed such a persistence to pray that thousands of years after the fact we not only know that he prayed, we know what he prayed. "...O that you would bless me and enlarge my territory! Let your hand be with me, and keep me from harm so that I will be free from pain." The interesting report of the historian follows. "And God granted his request." (1 Chronicles 4:10). That is the reward for persistent praying. Such praying is a prerequisite to praise. So, let us pray first, last, and always!

The Gratitude Attitude

The command "In everything give thanks" (1 Thessalonians 5:18*a*) has tripped a number of saints. Many respond by asking, "In everything?" The Bible says, "Yes, in everything!" I do not know of anyone who has learned to praise the Lord continuously who did not develop the gratitude attitude. The case for continuous thanksgiving cannot be overstated. It is a valuable part of mental, emotional, and spiritual health. C. S. Lewis said, "Praise is inner health made audible." But how does one develop the gratitude attitude? How does one take command of his or her emotions? The simple answer to that important question is—by obedience. Yes, we are simply to do as we are told.

It seems advisable here to point out a common misperception. Nowhere are we commanded to "feel grateful." Feelings are affected by the weather, the relative humidity, the temperature, the functions of one's liver, and who knows what else! Feelings are fickle. They come and go. They are also very unreliable reporters as to the true condition of things. We are commanded to "give thanks." There is no mention of feelings or assessments here. Giving thanks is an act of the will, of obedience. Few of us have any difficulty with the giving of thanks when all is going well. It is when the lights go out, health breaks down, matters go badly that we are mystified over the command to give thanks in all things. On what truth is such a seemingly unreasonable response predicated?

A couple of Scriptures will serve to answer this question. "And we know that in all things God works for the good of those who love him, who have been called according to his purpose" (Romans 8:28). The phrase "all things" is the foundation of our continuing thanksgiving. God's all-reaching and redemptive sovereignty is such that nothing can happen beyond His ability to make it a part in weaving the fabric of a meaningful and joyful life. His eternal providence renders it impossible that anything could ever happen that would not work together for our good. Isn't that thrilling? We don't have to merely grin and bear it, gritting our teeth and tolerating the circumstances. We can give thanks, knowing that the end result of the worst conditions will be our good and His glory!

Paul gives us more help as he writes the following instruction:

> All this is for your benefit, so that the grace that is reaching more and more people may cause thanksgiving to overflow to the glory of God. Therefore we do not lose heart. Though outwardly we are wasting away, yet inwardly we are being renewed day by day. For our light and momentary troubles are achieving for us an eternal glory that far outweighs them all. So we fix our eyes not on what is seen, but on what is unseen. For what is seen is temporary, but what is unseen is eternal (2 Corinthians 4:15-18).

Let's summarize what that passage teaches us:

1. What happens is for our benefit.
2. The result will be overflowing grace, causing thanksgiving.
3. Thanksgiving will bring glory to God.
4. Outwardly there is no reason for discouragement.
5. Inwardly there is spiritual renewal.
6. Our troubles are light and momentary.
7. It is those troubles, however, that are working for us a glory that greatly surpasses them.
8. We choose, then, to keep our eyes on the unseen reality rather than the seen. The former reality is eternal; the latter is temporary!

Therefore I may say of everything, "This is from God. It is for my benefit and for His glory. I choose to thank Him in all things. Thank you, Lord, for this gift. I receive it from You with gratitude that You will make it all that it was meant to be in eternity past."

An experience from my pastorate illustrates this. A dear lady in our church was informed that she had cancer. After she underwent surgery and subsequent treatments, the report seemed somewhat encouraging. My wife and I visited her at home. The room was dark and so were her spirits. We had not talked long before she said, somewhat apologetically, "Brother Jack, I know that you have always taught us to give thanks in all things, but I just can't give thanks in this matter!"

I asked why she could not give thanks, and her reply was, "I just don't feel grateful, and if I gave thanks, I would be a hypocrite." I reminded her that the Bible did not command her to feel grateful—but only to give thanks. It is not hypocritical to give thanks when you don't feel grateful. It is faith to give thanks when you feel nothing. It is an open declaration that you believe the Bible is right and that God is good and sovereign. After further clarification about the intent of the Scriptural command, I asked her, "Would you be willing simply to obey the Word?" I assured her it was as easy as saying, "Thank you!" We bowed our heads and prayed together. For the first time that dear lady thanked God in the midst of pain and puzzlement. When we left, the room was lighter, not only because the shades were raised and the curtains pulled, but because her heart had obeyed the Lord. Here is a helpful reminder: "When you don't feel like thanking God, thank God until you *feel* like thanking God—and then thank God some more!"

C. S. Lewis in his *Reflections on the Psalms* said the following:

> I had not noticed how the humblest, and the most balanced minds, praised most, while the cranks, misfits, and malcontents, praised least. The good critics found something to praise in the most imperfect works; the bad ones continually narrowed the list of books we might be allowed to read. The healthy and unaffected man, even if luxuriously brought up, could praise a very modest meal; the dyspeptic and the snob found fault with all.

Choose the path that leads to praise. Make the choice to rejoice. Pray persistently. Adopt the gratitude attitude. Having done so you will find yourself standing on the pinnacle of praise ready to cry out with the whole creation, "Let everything that has breath praise the Lord!"

Projects in Praise

1. Memorize 1 Thessalonians 5:16-18, our text for this chapter.
2. Be honest about tendencies in your life which are not in accord with the spirit of this passage.
3. Ask the Lord to remind you of anything for which you have not given thanks. Respond by repenting of the sin of disobedience and then give thanks obediently.
4. It is time to rehearse Psalm 119:164: "Seven times a day I praise you for your righteous laws." Remember that if you pray upon rising, upon going to bed, as you eat your three meals, and take a *praise break* in mid-morning and mid-afternoon, you will praise the Lord seven times. You will soon find yourself habitually praising the Lord.

The Pattern of Praise

A scene from Isaiah 6 should help us to explore the pattern of heavenly praise. It was the year 759 B.C. King Uzziah had died. Scripture indicates that King Uzziah's reign was characterized by as much blessing in greatness, splendor, and wealth as any king before him except Solomon. Few men can endure greatness, however, and before long pride and independence took their toll on Uzziah.

Uzziah was sixteen years old when he was made king, and he began his reign by seeking the Lord. He heeded instructions from Zechariah, the prophet, who coached him in the concerns of the Lord. We read of him, "As long as he sought the Lord, God gave him success" (2 Chronicles 26:5*b*) He defeated the Philistines, the Arabs, and the Meunites. He rebuilt cities, constructed towers in the desert, and owned herds of cattle on the plains and in the foothills. He developed a well-trained army prepared to do battle at a moment's notice. He made war machines designed for use in the towers of defense. His fame spread far and wide, even to the borders of Egypt. Such was the kingdom under mighty King Uzziah.

But as many men do, Uzziah forgot the source of his success—that it was God who gave him his greatness and could also take it from him. Second Chronicles 26:15*b* tells us of the tragic beginning of his downfall: "for he was greatly helped until he became powerful." His power was his undoing. The very next statement crowns the description: "But after Uzziah became powerful, his pride led to his downfall." His unfaithfulness to God was expressed as he presumptuously entered the Temple with a golden censer in his hand to burn incense. This privilege was reserved only for the consecrated priests. When the priests cautioned the king about the danger of his actions, he lost his temper and flew into a rage against them. Immediately he was smitten with leprosy, the most shameful disease of his day. He had leprosy until the day he died. Excluded from both palace and Temple, he lived in a separate house as a sad and sickly recluse.

It was in the year of Uzziah's death that Isaiah had his breath-taking vision. He found himself suddenly in the midst of a stirring worship service. He saw the Lord (Adonai) on a throne, high and exalted, the train of His robe filling the Temple. He then described strange creatures in attendance, whom he called *Seraphim.* This is the only time the word is used in the Bible, and it is somewhat mysterious. The word means *flaming ones.* These creatures possessed six wings. With one pair of wings, they covered their faces. With the second pair of wings, they covered their feet. With the remaining pair of wings, they flew about the throne. They called to one another, "Holy, holy, holy, is the Lord of hosts: the whole earth is full of his glory" (Isaiah 6:3, KJV). The sound of their voices caused the doorposts to shake, and the whole Temple was filled with smoke.

From this marvelous worship experience we begin to pick up a pattern or protocol of praise. This is, of course, a heavenly scene. It was not a figment of Isaiah's imagination or a product of indigestion. It was an opening into the realm of the unseen where Isaiah had a glimpse of reality. The sequel to this scene is found in Revelation 4, the subject of our discussion in Chapter 1. We need to view four elements of this episode.

Conditions Conducive to Seeing God

Times of tragedy particularly call for worship. The king was dead. He had reigned for fifty-two years, and in a way, his death was a climax to a national tragedy. When God had smitten him with leprosy, he was not dead and thus could not be mourned. His son, Jotham, had charge of the palace and governed the people but was not the king. The king had no fellowship with his people. He was soon a forgotten man except when someone asked about him and then the answer was, "He has leprosy." God has been known to empty thrones, chairs, or homes that He may reveal Himself. When the earthly king was dead, Isaiah, and thus the people, had a glimpse of the Heavenly King.

A View of the One Worshipped

Isaiah had no description of God as such in his vision. He did describe the regal splendor of God's surroundings, including the fact that God was on a throne. We have little appreciation for thrones and their significance in our Western world. In days of old, the higher and greater the throne, the greater the personage who sat upon it. God was on a throne, high and lifted up. This throne, doubtless the same throne described by John in Revelation 4, is the real throne of the universe. A greater than Uzziah or Solomon in all their earthly glory, is seated upon it. The length of the royal robe was also a measure of the magnitude of greatness. The greatness of this King was such that His train "filled the temple." He is *Adonai*, the One who rules. Never had Isaiah seen such a king!

A View of the Ones Worshipping

The mystery of the seraphim will not be settled until we worship at that same throne in heaven, but their actions give us some vital implications regarding the protocol of worship. The throne is the center of their attention. Both their posture and their conversation are worthy of note. With one pair of wings they covered their faces, symbolizing reverence. They could not look on the greatness of the Shining One who sat upon the throne. With a second pair of wings, they covered their feet, a sign of humility. With the pair remaining, they flew, signifying service and obedience. They were praising God.

Their first words were almost identical to those spoken by the living creatures of Revelation 4, "Holy, holy, holy, Lord God Almighty...(KJV)" This is the central attribute of God. He is holy. He is flawless and spotless. There is nothing of Him for anyone to criticize. He is beyond scrutiny! He is *El Shaddai*, the Mighty One able to nourish and provide. The voices of the Seraphim are loud, so loud that the portals of the doors shake and tremble. For those who detest loud praises, here is a caution. We have recorded here the protocol of heaven. Who are we to decide what is proper deportment before the throne of God?

Biblical praise can often become noisy! It is not uncommon in Revelation for the praises to be described *in a loud voice.* In Revelation 5:11-12 there is a description of angels numbering "thousands upon thousands, and ten thousand times ten thousand … in a loud voice they sang ..." In Revelation 7:10 a great multitude which no man could count "cried out in a loud voice; 'Salvation belongs to our God, who sits on the throne, and to the Lamb.'" In Revelation 12 after the great dragon who had made war in heaven was hurled down to the earth, a loud voice announced, "Now have come the salvation and the power and the kingdom of our God, and the authority of his Christ." (v. 10). The four "hallelujahs" in Revelation 19 were all loud like the roar of a vast multitude (v. 1); they repeated it (v. 3 and 4); "like a great multitude, like the roar of rushing waters and like loud peals of thunder, shouting ..." (v. 6).

A View of the One Viewing the Worship Scene

At first Isaiah was a spectator. But we cannot remain spectators for long in a genuine scene of worship. Soon our turn will come to respond. In such a scene, before each individual has time to pass judgment, he or she is judged! There are three rhyming words which hint at what happens in the midst of heavenly praise.

The first word is *woe.* This is a word of conviction and confession. A proper self-assessment is always afforded in an atmosphere of praise. "I am ruined!" exclaimed Isaiah. Then he became rather specific, "I am a man of unclean lips, and I live among a people of unclean lips..."(Isaiah 6:5) It is not unusual for conviction to break out during a service of heavenly worship. Sometimes stern preaching brings conviction. There are other times when the greatest conviction is produced by praise.

Some time ago, I was in a meeting that turned into a revival. On the second night of the meeting the pastor made a rather shocking disclosure. He confessed that he had not been scripturally baptized and had been guilty of covering his sin. He then proceeded to offer himself as a candidate for baptism. His obedience and candid honesty broke the meeting open and dozens began to respond. The meeting, scheduled for four days, continued for fourteen days. ***After the second night, praise brought about more conviction and decisions than did preaching and pleading.*** In fact, night after night we would gather and praise the Lord in song and testimony for an hour or more. I announced my preaching was not an end in itself but a means to an end. It would do little good for me to complicate the situation further if the people were already prepared to obey God. When I then gave an invitation without preaching, people came and came and came. Praise both preceded and pervaded the entire proceedings of that meeting. One night a visitor walked into the atmosphere of praise and immediately fell under conviction of a personal sin. Not one word was spoken about that sin, but at the first opportunity he publicly repented.

So it was with Isaiah. No one pointed out his sin, but there was something about the praise which exalted a holy God that brought conviction, which resulted in both a personal and corporate confession.

The second word is *lo* (Isaiah 6:7, KJV). Isaiah had seen the King, the Lord Almighty, and conviction had come. In the vision, one of the seraphim came to Isaiah with a live coal from the altar. The seraph said, "Lo, this hath touched thy lips; and thine iniquity is taken away, and thy sin purged" (KJV). This is the word of divine cleansing. Conviction had ushered in confession and confession had given way to cleansing.

The third word is *go*. This is a word of service. Praise which does not lead to sanctified service has not been genuine praise. Immediately after the cleansing experience with the live coal on Isaiah's lips, the Lord is heard to inquire, "Whom shall I send, and who will go for us?" Isaiah responds quickly: "Here am I. Send me!" (v. 8) Genuine worship and praise evokes and intensifies commitment, consecration, and obedience.

Over seven centuries later, John on Patmos Isle walked into that same worship service! Could it be that there is an eternal worship service going on, and every now and then someone is blessed with the privilege of being included? Paul reminds us in Romans 1:25 that God is "forever praised." The creatures in Revelation 4 also have six wings and "Day and night they never stop saying, 'Holy, holy, holy is the Lord God Almighty, who was, and is, and is to come.'"

My conviction is that this service of worshipful adoration and praise is still in session. God is continuously being praised. We line up with eternal and invisible reality when we praise.

Our testimony will likely be similar to Isaiah's on praise: *I saw the Lord. I witnessed the praise. I was convicted, and I confessed: I was cleansed. I heard the call, and I made the commitment.*

Projects in Praise

1. Compare the scene of Isaiah 6 with that of Revelation 4.
   A. Compare and contrast the descriptions of God.
   B. Compare and contrast the descriptions of the throne.
   C. Compare and contrast the descriptions of the worshipping ones.
2. Memorize both the worship declaration of the seraphim in Isaiah 6 and the living creatures of Revelation 4.
   Holy, holy, holy is the Lord Almighty;
   the whole earth is full of his glory (Isaiah 6:3).
   Holy, holy, holy is the Lord God Almighty,
   who was, and is, and is to come (Revelation 4:8*b*).
3. Memorize the response of the twenty-four elders in Revelation 4:11:
   You are worthy, our Lord and God, to receive
   glory and honor and power, for you created all
   things, and by your will they were created and
   have their being.
4. Use all the above in your personal praises today.
5. Remember to program your "praise breaks" into your day. These are ideal passages to use in your praises to God.

The Premier Word for Praise: Hallelujah!

Hallelujah in the Old Testament

We will discover that the word most often used for praise in the Old Testament was *hallal*. (This is the English pronunciation of the Hebrew word.) We will study this word more fully in our next chapter. There are many different words used in the Hebrew language which have been rendered "praise" in our English translations. Without the aid of the Hebrew we would mistakenly assume that there was only one word in the original language to denote praise. The truth is that there are more than fifty such words! Many of them will be dealt with later on, but for now I want to treat a remarkable word derived from *hallal*, the most commonly used word for praise in our Bible. (It is used some ninety-nine times!)

The word I'm speaking of is *hallelujah*. The Hebrew word *hallal* forms the first part of this splendid word which I have labeled the premier word for praise. I am told that this word has transcended the language barrier among the major languages of the world. Because of the providence of God, I believe, the original word has such majesty and completeness that instead of being translated, it was transliterated. Thus, in English it is pronounced *hallelujah*; in Italian it is pronounced *hallelujah*; in Spanish it is pronounced *hallelujah*, and so on.

We have in this marvelous word a combination of two Hebrew words. The first, *hallal*, means "to boast, to brag on, to laud, to make a show, even to the point of looking foolish." The second, *Jah*, is simply the shortened name for God. Thus, *hallelujah* became the spontaneous outcry of one excited about God, the exclamation of one upon whose consciousness part of the majesty of God has dawned. Although *hallal* is found ninety-nine times in the Old Testament, the word *hallelujah* is used only twenty-four times—all of them in the Psalms, occurring between Psalm 104 and Psalm 150. The distinction, I believe, is worthy of note. Hallelujah seems to be reserved as a special response of extreme excitement, exuberance, and exultation.

What are we expressing about life, about man, about history, and about God when we say *hallelujah*—or *praise the Lord* as many versions translate the word? How are we affected? Why is it vital in corporate worship and private worship? None of these questions may be answered in a complete sense this side of heaven, but some answers seem implied in Scripture. Please read the following verses:

> Psalms 104:35; 105:45; 106:1,48; 111:1; 112:1; 113:1,9; 115:18; 116:19; 117:2; 135:1,3,21; 146:1,10; 147:1,20; 148:1,14; 149:1,9; 150:1,6.

It is further interesting and revealing to note the following:

Two psalms begin with *hallelujah* (Psalm 111 and Psalm 112). Five psalms end with *hallelujah* (Psalm 104, Psalm 105, Psalm 115, Psalm 116, and Psalm 117). Eight psalms begin and end with *hallelujah* (Psalm 106, Psalm 113, Psalm 135, Psalms 146-150). Only one psalm (Psalm 135) contains *hallelujah* within it (v. 3).

A careful examination of the glorious truths contained within the framework of these twenty-four usages of *hallelujah* may give us helpful clues toward answering the question, "Why *hallelujah*?"

It Has the Ring of Purpose and Providence

There are manifold mentions in the "Hallelujah Psalms" of the purpose of God. He is seen in these Psalms working from a purpose, with a purpose, and toward a purpose.

First, there is His purpose in creation. In Psalm 104 He wraps Himself in light and stretches out the heavens like a tent (v. 2). He lays the beams of His upper chambers on the waters and makes the clouds His chariot, riding on the wings of the wind (v. 3). He makes winds His messengers and flames of fire His servants (v. 4). He has established the earth and it cannot be moved (v. 5). The remainder of Psalm 104 shows God controlling the waters, the grass, the beasts, the birds, the moon, the sun, the sea creatures, the earth, and the mountains. In the midst of it the psalmist exclaims, "How many are your works, O Lord! In wisdom you made them all; the earth is full of your creatures" (v. 24).

Psalm 105 and Psalm 106 contain references to the manner in which God used His sovereign power in the lives of His people. He called famine on the land (Psalm 105:16). The judgments upon Egypt exhibited His control of the elements in His vast creation. He sent darkness (Psalm 105:28). He turned their waters to blood (Psalm 105:29). He spoke and swarms of flies and gnats came upon the land (Psalm 105:31). He turned the rain to hail and commanded the locusts to devour the land (Psalm 105:32-35). He brought a cloud to cover them by day and a fire to comfort them by night (Psalm 105:39). He produced quail when they asked and provided their daily manna (Psalm 105:40). The waters of the Red Sea parted for God's people at His command and came back to cover their enemies (Psalm 106:9-11).

Psalm 135 contains the testimony of God having His way in the heavens, earth, and in the seas (vv. 6-7). Again, in Psalm 147, we behold God covering the sky with clouds, supplying the earth with rain, and making grass to grow on the hills (v. 8). He spreads the snow across the earth and scatters the frost like ashes, hurls down the hail like stones, sends His word and melts it, and stirs up His breezes (vv. 16-18).

Psalm 148 is a veritable roll call of creation. Everything is commanded to praise the Lord. No less than twenty-two personages, animals, and elements of creation are called upon to praise the Lord. The angels, the heavenly hosts, the sun, moon, stars, highest heavens, waters above the skies, sea creatures, ocean depths, lightning, hail, snow, clouds, stormy winds, mountains, hills, fruit trees, cedars, wild animals, cattle, small creatures, and flying birds are commanded to praise the Lord! All of this is sandwiched between two ringing hallelujah's! The remainder of Psalm 148 calls upon people of the earth to praise God. The fact that all of creation answers to God and responds to His beckoning seems to be a reason for shouting hallelujah.

God's Purposes: Blessings

Second, in the "Hallelujah Psalms" we view God's purposes as they relate to Israel. The descendants of Abraham and Jacob are called upon in Psalm 105 to remember the wonders, miracles, and judgments (vv. 5,6). The remainder of the chapter is an outline of God's covenant dealings with his people, coming to a climax in verses 43-45:

> He brought out his people with rejoicing, his chosen ones with shouts of joy; he gave them the lands of the nations, and they fell heir to what others had toiled for—that they might keep his precepts and observe his laws.

Then another *hallelujah* is sounded!

Psalm 106, beginning and ending in a *hallelujah* is an account of Israel's deliverance, backslidings, murmurings, idol worship, wasting in sin, and God's disciplinary actions. Then comes a cry at the end of the psalm:

> Save us, O Lord our God, and gather us from the nations that we may give thanks to your name and glory in your praise. Praise be to the Lord, the God of Israel, from everlasting to everlasting. Let all the people say, "Amen!" Praise the Lord [Hallelujah] (vv. 47-48).

In Psalm 112 the purposes of God extend beyond Israel to anyone who "fears the Lord, who finds great delight in his commands" (v. 1). The remainder of Psalm 112 lists the dividends that accrue to such actions. His children will be mighty; wealth and riches will be in his house; stability will be his lot; bad news will not come to him; he will be fearless; his righteousness will endure; and his enemies will view it and be vexed. This was all prefaced by a *hallelujah*!

In Psalm 113 *hallelujah's* flank the good news that God raises the poor from the dust and lifts the needy from the ash heap, seating them among princes. The barren woman He makes a happy mother.

In Psalm 115 (which ends in hallelujah) God's blessings are pronounced on the house of Israel and the house of Aaron.

Again in Psalm 135 (the only psalm with three *hallelujah*'s) God's dealings with Israel are extolled, especially the havoc He wrought on Egypt by His signs and wonders (vv. 8 and 9). On Israel's behalf He had struck down nations and kings and given their land as an inheritance to His people, Israel (vv. 8-12). The houses of Israel, Aaron, and Levi are admonished to praise the Lord. Then it is hallelujah time again in the final statement of the psalm.

God's purposes for His people are further revealed in Psalm 146, and He is faithful to His purposes.

> He upholds the cause of the oppressed and gives food to the hungry. The Lord sets the prisoners free, the Lord gives sight to the blind, the Lord lifts up those who are bowed down, the Lord loves the righteous. The Lord watches over the alien and sustains the fatherless and the widow, but he frustrates the ways of the wicked (vv. 7-9).

It Has the Ring of Power and Sovereignty

Through this series of Psalms there is a constant sounding of God's might and limitless abilities. "O Lord my God, you are very great; you are clothed with splendor and majesty," exclaimed the psalmist in Psalm 104:1. In Psalm 106:2 he asks, "Who can proclaim the mighty acts of the Lord or fully declare his praise?" He further declares, "Great are the works of the Lord; they are pondered by all who delight in them. Glorious and majestic are his deeds, and his righteousness endures forever" (Psalm 111:2-3).

Hallelujah seems to be the only response that is reasonable in the light of God's greatness. "The Lord is exalted over all the nations, his glory above the heavens. Who is like the Lord our God, the One who sits enthroned on high, who stoops down to look on the heavens and the earth?" (Psalm 113:4-6)

Early on in Psalm 115 there is a study in contrasts of the God of Israel and the idols of the heathen. God does whatever He pleases. The idols have mouths but cannot speak, eyes but cannot see, noses but cannot smell, hands but cannot feel, feet but cannot walk. The God of Israel deserves glory and honor (115:1,18).

That comparison, in part, is repeated in Psalm 135:15-18. In verse 13 the psalmist breaks into praise with these words, "Your name, O Lord, endures forever, your renown, O Lord, through all generations." The continuing theme in the "Hallelujah Psalms" is the greatness of God.

The crescendo rises in the latter psalms, climaxing in Psalm 150 with: "Praise him for his acts of power; praise him for his surpassing greatness" (v. 2).

It Has the Ring of Permanence

Hallelujah is inescapably eternal. When we say it, sing it, or shout it, we are aligning with eternity. Listen to the ring of eternity in these psalms:

> May the glory of the Lord endure *forever*...(Psalm 104:31).
> Praise be to the Lord, the God of Israel, from *everlasting to everlasting* (Psalm 106:48*a*).
> His righteousness endures *forever*... he remembers his covenant *forever*... the works of his hands are faithful and just; all his precepts are trustworthy. They are steadfast *forever* and ever, done in faithfulness and uprightness...he ordained his covenant *forever*... To him belongs eternal praise (Psalm 111:3*b*-10).
> Let the name of the Lord be praised both *now and forevermore* (Psalm 113:2).
> It is we who extol the Lord both *now and forevermore* (Psalm 115:18).
> For great is his love toward us, and the faithfulness of the Lord endures *forever* (Psalm 117:2).
> Your name, O Lord, endures *forever*, your renown, O Lord, *through all generations* (Psalm 135:13).
> The Lord reigns *forever*, your God, O Zion, *for all generations* (Psalm 146:10).

Have you noticed how many verses speak of eternity in the environment of *hallelujah*? *Hallelujah* brings us to breathe the air of heaven, accords the greatness due God's name, and affords us a view of God as He is and things as they are.

Hallelujah resounds ten times in Psalms 146-150. Ultimately everything in creation is ordered to praise the Lord. All the elements, plant and animal life, princes and kings of the earth, all musical instruments, and "everything that has breath" will praise the Lord. The final, triumphant note is appropriately ... *Hallelujah!*

Projects in Praise

1. Read carefully all the psalms which contain *hallelujah*.
2. Use the word *hallelujah* to preface a characteristic of God referred to in these psalms.
3. In your seven "praise breaks" try using *hallelujah* each time in extolling God's virtues.
4. Memorize one of the last five psalms (Psalms 146-150) and utilize it in your personal time of praise each day.
5. Review your memory work of the past projects.

The Premier Word for Praise: Hallelujah!

Hallelujah in the New Testament

We observed in the previous chapter that the premier word for praise, *hallelujah*, was used twenty-four times in the Old Testament. In few translations, however, do we find it rendered *hallelujah*, rather than simply "Praise the Lord." The Amplified Bible, translates it *hallelujah* in all its occurrences.

The New Testament uses *hallelujah* even more sparingly—only four times, in fact. Yet the usages are worthy of study, for we have unveiled in them more of the mysteries of this amazing word. All the *hallelujah*'s in the New Testament are found in Revelation 19. Let us view the four *hallelujah*'s of the Revelation.

Historical Setting

In Revelation 17 John was shown a woman—a prostitute—sitting on a scarlet beast. Regardless of one's persuasion as to the meaning of the Revelation, there is rather common agreement that this symbolizes a world system in which religious and political powers have joined hands. The prostitute has mighty power among the nations of the world. She has seduced the kings of the earth and wields mighty authority over nations. The beast upon which she sat had seven heads and ten horns. The heads stood for seven hills or seven kings under the prostitute. The ten horns (a horn generally symbolizes power) are ten kingdoms that will be empowered along with the beast. They have one purpose, to make war against the Lamb. Of course, the Lamb will overcome them because He is none other than the Lord of lords and King of kings.

In Revelation 18 is recorded the destruction of the total world system, *Babylon*. Her productivity is terminated, and the merchants of the earth weep over her fall. God's judgment is complete and sudden. "In one hour she has been brought to ruin!" (Revelation 18:19*b*). Her final benediction is sounded in the closing verses of Revelation 18:

> The music of harpists and musicians, flute players and trumpeters, will never be heard in you again. No workmen of any trade will ever be found in you again. The sound of a millstone will never be heard in you again. The light of a lamp will never shine in you again. The voice of bridegroom and bride will never be heard in you again. Your merchants were the world's great men. By your magic spell all the nations were led astray. In her was found the blood of prophets and of the saints, and of all who have been killed on the earth (vv. 22-24).

This is the background against which are sounded the four *hallelujah*'s of Revelation 19.

The Hallelujah of Redemption Crowned

"After this ....," John writes, "I heard what sounded like the roar of a great multitude in heaven shouting." It was after the vision of the total destruction of the world system that this sound issued from heaven. Evidently the shouts from heaven are in response to what has taken place on the earth. Their shout is, "Hallelujah! Salvation, and glory, and power belong to our God, for true and just are his judgments." *Salvation* has been manifested in total deliverance. God has revealed His glory, and the arm of His power has been mighty. His justice has been displayed upon the earth. He who initiated the redemption of His people will bring it to consummation. No wonder that heaven should join in one great hallelujah! It matters not what history looks like from the current and visible viewpoint. It is the final state of affairs which matters most. And here we have it. We have read the last chapter and we win. We win because He won! Hallelujah!

The Hallelujah of Retribution Complete

Any system of justice deals with both retribution and reward. It is exceedingly difficult to stand by on earth, realizing what we know about the absolute truths of God, and see injustice parade under the guise of enlightenment. The gross violation of civil rights by heartless despots and the slaughter of millions of innocent, unborn children are only a part of the tragic picture. The arrogant tyrants seem unchecked in their ill-conceived plans to control the earth. The score seems to be highly in favor of the world system. Hope is not dead, though. There is a sound coming from heaven. The hosts of heaven are shouting, "'He has condemned the great prostitute who corrupted the earth by her adulteries. He has avenged on her the blood of his servants.' And again they shouted: 'Hallelujah! The smoke from her goes up for ever and ever.'"

There is revenge upon the harlot. The saints have been avenged. The judge of the earth will not allow one injustice to go unpunished. His system of retribution is geared to His sovereignty. All will be equalized in the end. The angels rejoice here because they have been observing unpunished injustices, wickedness prospering, evil triumphing, and unchecked immorality. Meanwhile, the righteous suffer, good causes go begging, and honor and honesty go unrewarded. Now the accounts will be settled. Every drop of blood that was shed in injustice will be avenged. The scales of eternal justice will be in perfect balance! God will have settled the score. When the hosts of heaven see the world system—the prostitute—being punished, they shout with joy, "Hallelujah!"

The Hallelujah of the Reign Confirmed

The scene changes somewhat and the twenty-four elders and the four living creatures (the ones we met in Revelation 4) are seen to fall down and worship God, with the exclamation, "Amen, hallelujah!" With a fresh revelation of the mightiness of God, there is a new sense of His sovereignty. This is familiar territory. We are back where we began. The fact that God reigns elicits from earth and heaven a loud shout of praise. The command goes forth, "Praise our God, all you his servants, you who fear him, both small and great!" (v. 5).

We cannot remain in our aloofness as spectators in such surroundings as these! We must prepare to sound with them the final shout.

The Hallelujah of Relationship Consummated

Now, more loudly than ever, they shout from heaven, "like a great multitude, like the roar of rushing waters, like loud peals of thunder" (v. 6). We come here to the final *hallelujah* of the Bible. One consummate *hallelujah* is reserved for the great coming event of history when the Bride and Bridegroom will be joined in eternal union at the marriage of the Lamb. God reigns! We are to rejoice and be glad and give him the glory. It's wedding time and the Bride is ready. As we look about us we are haunted by the unpreparedness of the Bride. But our collective spines should tingle at the thought that there will be a time in the future when she *will* be ready. The reign of our God will give way to the rejoicing of God's people. And we rejoice with reason—it's our wedding day! The wedding apparel is in place. It is "fine linen, bright and clean" (v. 8). The fine linen represents the righteous acts of the saints. The relationship is consummated. The bride-elect becomes the Bride indeed. She is seated next to her Bridegroom-Lord and will at His side exercise authority with Him for all eternity. Surely *hallelujah* is in order at prospects such as these.

The "Hallelujah Chorus"

Most of us are familiar to some degree with the musical masterpiece *Messiah*. Few may remember, however, the circumstances which brought it about. In 1741, the 57-year-old Handel's personal life was in a sad state. He was hopelessly in debt and in a severe depression. Hope for recovery seemed faint indeed. About this time a minor poet, by the name of Charles Jenners, delivered to Handel a collection of Biblical excerpts under the title of *A Sacred Oratorio*. With little interest, George Fredrick Handel began to turn the leaves of the manuscript, "He was despised and rejected of men." The heart of Handel found sympathy, for, he too, was "despised and rejected of men" Something began to happen to him. The words began to reverberate in his soul: "Wonderful, Counselor, the Mighty God, the Everlasting Father, the Prince of Peace." He began to compose a setting for these magnificent words, remaining in seclusion for twenty-four days! Sometimes his food was untouched. At times he would jump up and wave his hands in the air, shouting, "Hallelujah!" Later Handel confided, "I think I did see all heaven before me, and the great God Himself." The result is history, and thousands of times each Christmas and Easter season since then, crowds have been inspired by the masterpiece which climaxes in the great "Hallelujah Chorus." At one of the earlier performances in

London, as the crescendo of the musical rose with the "Hallelujah Chorus" the king stood and all the audience with him. It has been accepted procedure since that time to stand for this famous chorus.

Why Hallelujah?

We have not exhausted, by any means, the deep mysteries of the premier word for praise, but we may now have an idea about why we use it. Hallelujah looks in all directions. It looks backward to the beginning of salvation and forward to salvation crowned. It looks upward to God enthroned and downward to the devil enchained. It looks inward to fear diminished and faith established. It looks outward to righteousness and readiness. Hallelujah!

Projects in Praise

1. Our projects center around *hallelujah.* Memorize Revelation 19:6*b*-7 (the final hallelujah).
2. Investigate the use of the word *hallelujah* in the hymnal which your congregation uses.
3. Memorize at least two verses of a hymn which uses the word and utilize it in your personal worship time.
4. Remain faithful in your "praise breaks" (seven times a day).
5. Review your previous praise projects and follow through on them.

Songs Using Hallelujah:

"All Creatures of Our God and King"
"Praise My Soul, the King of Heaven"
"Come Christians, Join to Sing"
"The Strife is O'er"
"Our Lord Christ Hath Risen"
"Low in the Grave He Lay" ("Christ Arose")
"Hallelujah! Christ is Risen"
"Christ the Lord Is Risen Today"
"It May Be at Morn"
"He is Coming!"
"Revive Us Again"
"Satisfied"
"Mine Eyes Have Seen the Glory"

Sample verse:

Praise my soul, the King of Heaven,
To His feet thy tribute bring;
Ransomed, sealed, restored, forgiven,
Evermore His praises sing:

Hallelujah, Hallelujah
Praise the Everlasting King.

10 Praise: A Word Study in Hebrew

As we delve beneath the surface of the English words pertaining to praise, we will find bountiful treasures that will make our word study more than worthwhile. I have found myself returning again and again to the research on original word studies to enhance my study of certain Scriptures regarding praise.

In the providence of God, the Scriptures came to us in their original form in Hebrew and Greek. I would not for a moment want to leave the impression that one must understand these languages to understand the Bible. That would be an unfortunate impression and untrue; but I do want to insist, on the other hand, that observations of original word meanings can provide valuable insights and can serve to increase our understanding and appreciation of our English words.

With an immediate awareness of my incompetence in the original languages, especially Hebrew, I called upon a seminary professor and sought to employ him in the research. With deadlines facing him on other projects he declined but recommended a young man to do the work in research, referring to him as the most brilliant young linguist he knew. Dr. Robert D. Bergen was contacted and an agreement was immediately reached and the assignment given. Within seven days from the first contact, a thorough study in both Hebrew and Greek was handed to me. The following materials are a result of that research. Again, I sense the need to remind the reader, especially the layperson, that this material needs to be approached as more technical than inspirational. If that is kept in mind, it will not be readily laid aside because of the lack of its emotional appeal. On the other hand, it will be respected as necessary foundation material to support the practice of praise from the Biblical standpoint.

We have already observed that more than fifty words are

used in the Hebrew language in connection with praise. While these are different words, I do not mean to imply that they are unrelated. The fact is that many of them are derivatives of one root word. Considering this, I will use the following format: The words will be presented from the most frequently used to the least used. I will give the English pronunciation and the meaning of the term. Then I will list Scriptures in which that word is used. This will enable the reader to mark in his or her own Bible the various shades of the meaning of praise.

Hallal

We have met this word before. From it is derived the word I have referred to as the premier word for praise in the Bible—Hallelujah. *Hallal* is used ninety-nine times in the Old Testament, more than any of the other major words translated "praise." Almost one third of the occurrences of this word are in the Psalms and are summons to praise. The word means "to laud, to boast, to celebrate, to be clamorously foolish." One cannot help being reminded of "first love" between a boy and a girl. There is a point at which reason seems to be loosed from its moorings and the emotions soar. There is also a point at which praise seems too little concerned with reason and intellect and could be labeled by the watching skeptic as "foolish."

Twenty-four times this word is employed with the name of God, *Jah*, to form the premier word for praise. These references are noted in Chapter 8. If you have not already noted these special usages in your Bible, stop your reading and do so now.

Key Passages Using *Hallal*

He [David] appointed some of the Levites to minister before the ark of the Lord, to make petition, to give thanks, and to praise [*hallal*] the Lord, the God of Israel (1 Chronicles 16:4).

When I am afraid, I will trust in you. In God, whose word I praise [*hallal*], in God I trust; I will not be afraid. What can mortal man do to me? In God's word I praise [*hallal*], in the Lord whose word I praise [*hallal*] (Psalm 56:3,4,10).

Blessed are those who dwell in your house; they are ever praising [*hallal*] you (Psalm 84:4).

Let this be written for a future generation, that a people not yet created may praise [*hallal*] the Lord (Psalm 102:18).

From the rising of the sun to the place where it sets the name of the Lord is to be praised [*hallal*] (Psalm 113:3).

> Seven times a day I praise [*hallal*] you for your righteous laws (Psalm 119:164).

These are a few of many references in the Scriptures. We will view more of these when we make reference to Scriptures where more than one word is used for praise in the same passage. See Appendix E for a longer list of references you may want to use as you do your own study on praise.

Yadah

This word is the next most frequently translated "praise" in the Old Testament. The word means "to worship with extended hands, to throw out the hands, to give thanks to God." It is often rendered "thanks" or "thanksgiving" in the English translations. It is obvious from verses in the Old Testament that the lifting of the hands was of some significance in worship.

Few exercises in worship today are more controversial than the lifting of the hands, unless it is the open use of glossalalia! It seems to be most offensive to those who have never done it. Let us view some references to this act of hand-lifting. Psalm 134:2 enjoins us to "lift up our hands in the sanctuary and bless the Lord." In Nehemiah 8:6 we see that "all the people lifted their hands and responded, 'Amen! Amen!'" The psalmist declared in Psalm 63:4, "I will praise you as long as I live, and in your name I will lift up my hands." Paul, in 1 Timothy 2:8, states, "I want men everywhere to lift up holy hands in prayer, without anger or disputing." I want to be frank with you, understanding the risk of offense. This exercise is one of the most explosive and meaningful expressions of praise! **I believe that God loves it, the flesh hates it, and the devil is devastated by it.** I believe that with its exercise, faith stands firm, fear takes flight, and joy takes hold. Our hands are an inevitable part of almost every response pattern. They are a means of extending our emotions, as well as expressing our emotions.

I have been told that the raising of the hands is an international sign of surrender. While this may be significant, I believe that it fails to capture the essence of its meaning. I happen to be a delighted, doting, captivated, adoring grandfather. It was love before first sight. I have never had an experience just like it. I do not remember having the time or sense to love my own children as much as I do my granddaughter. I loved her before I knew that she was a *she!* I loved her before she knew how to respond to that love; however, as she learned to respond—first with a smile, then a giggle, then open laughter—she was an ever-increasing delight to me. How happy was that day, now long ago, when she held those dimpled little hands up toward Grandpa. She had not a word, just this simple gesture. I didn't have to consult the dictionary, an encyclopedia, a sociologist, or a psychologist. I knew what she was saying. It was as clear as it could be. She was saying, "I want to come to you. I want you to take me in your arms. I like it there. We will have fun together. I like what happens to me when I am with you. I accept your love for me." Now, could you guess what my response was? You don't need three chances, do you? Well, I didn't say, "Stop that, you little charismatic! You're just showing off and trying to embarrass me!" I grabbed her forthwith and obliged her request for a place in my arms!

Since that time, as I have lifted my hands to the Lord in private worship (and sometimes in public!), the exercise means even more to me. I am saying to the Lord, "Father, I want you, I receive you, I yield to you. I like what I feel when I am with you. Take me." If you think that is cheap emotionalism, just leave me alone in it. I like it both with my granddaughter and the Lord!

The word *yadah* is used over ninety times in the Old Testament. My conviction is that we may safely assume that this particular reference to praise involves thanksgiving to God accompanied by uplifted hands.

It might be added that the root of the word *yadah* is *yad*, which means "hand" and thus—in the lengthened form—is translated "to throw, to cast, or to shoot." It is translated in the King James Version "praise" fifty-three times, "give thanks" thirty-two times, "thank" five times, and "confess" sixteen times.

Key Passages Using *Yadah*

Genesis 29:35*; 2 Chronicles 20:21; Psalm 9:1; 52:9; 107:8,15,21,31; 139:14; 145:10.

*This is the occasion of the birth of Leah's fourth son by Jacob, whom she called "Judah"—meaning "praise the Lord."

Barak

Barak is a vital word connected with praise in the Old Testament. Its uniqueness is enhanced when we discover that it is translated "praise" only rarely in the King James Version. The New International Version, my principal source, regularly translates it "praise." *Barak* is used over 200 times to denote blessing or blessings from God, as well as between people. Approximately seventy times it denotes praise to God. Harris, in his *Theological Wordbook of the Old Testament* indicates that it means "to kneel, to bless, to salute," or in rare instances, "to curse." Some feel that, since it is translated "to kneel" in certain cases, it may be related to *berek*, meaning "knee." The cases where *barak* is translated "praise" in the King James Version are Judges 5:2 and Psalm 72:15. The occasion of the first reference is the song of Deborah and Barak (whose very name means "bless"). Their song began with these words, "Praise [*barak*] ye the Lord for the avenging of Israel, when the people willingly offered themselves." The other reference in Psalm 72:15 is to Solomon, as the psalmist says, "And he shall live, and to him shall be given of the gold of Sheba: prayer also shall be made for him continually; and daily shall he be praised [*barak*]."

There are several key references worthy of special notice. When David was raising the monies and materials for building the Temple, and after he had given from his own personal treasures a vast amount of gold and silver, we find that "Wherefore David blessed [*barak*] the Lord before all the congregation" (1 Chronicles 29:10, KJV). The New International Version translates *barak* as "praise" in this verse. "David praised the Lord in the presence of the whole assembly, saying, 'Praise be to you, O Lord, God of our father Israel…'" (v. 11).

Best-known References to *Barak* as Praise in the Old Testament

The Lord gave and the Lord has taken away; may the name of the Lord be praised [*barak*] (Job 1:21*b*).

Sing praises to the Lord, praise [*barak*] his name; proclaim his salvation day after day (Psalm 96:2).

Praise [*barak*] the Lord, O my soul; all my inmost being, praise [*barak*] his holy name. Praise [*barak*] the Lord, O my soul, and forget not all his benefits (Psalm 103:1,2).

Praise [*barak*] the Lord, you his angels, you mighty ones who do his bidding, who obey his word. Praise [*barak*] the Lord, all his heavenly hosts, you his servants who do his will. Praise [*barak*] the Lord, all his works everywhere in his dominion. Praise [barak] the Lord, O my soul. (Psalm 103:20-22).

Praise [*barak*] the Lord, O my soul. O Lord, my God, you are very great; you are clothed with splendor and majesty (Psalm 104:1).

Other references for *barak* may be found in Appendix E.

A Final Word on *Barak*

We are often called on to give testimony of the Lord's blessings to us, and we should never be without a word in regard to this. However, it must be remembered that even here it is more blessed to give than to receive (Acts 20:35). That I can receive a blessing from the Lord is a welcome prospect. That I can both be and give a blessing to the Lord is even more thrilling. If David blessed the Lord, so can you and I. If it is a blessing to receive a blessing, it is a double blessing to give a blessing. *Barak* is one of the vital words pertaining to praise because it suggests that transcendent privilege of blessing the Lord.

Tehillah

Tehillah is the fourth most frequently used word relating to praise in the Old Testament, occurring over fifty times. It is derived from *hallal* and is generally accepted to mean the singing of *Hallal*'s. The word means "to sing or to laud." It is perceived as involving music, especially singing. Singing has always been vital in the worship of God. Aside from this word which involves singing, there are eight different Hebrew words translated "praise" in the King James Version. There are over 300 mandates in the Bible to sing. Obviously then, singing is a vital and indispensable form of praise.

Significant Usages of *Tehillah* in the Old Testament

But thou art holy, O thou that inhabitest the praises [*tehillah*] of Israel (Psalm 22:3, KJV).

Praise the Lord. [Hallelujah–from *hallal*] How good it is to sing praises [*zamar*–which I will cover later in this chapter] to our God, how pleasant and fitting to praise [*tehillah*] him (Psalm 147:1,2).

Who among the gods is like you, O Lord? Who is like you … majestic in holiness, awesome in glory [*tehillah*], working wonders? (Exodus 15:11) KJV translates this "fearful in praises."

He is your praise [*tehillah*]: he is your God, who performed for you those great and awesome wonders you saw with your own eyes (Deuteronomy 10:21).

The above Scripture suggests that God Himself is our song of praise. This agrees with the word of Moses and the Israelites in Exodus 15:2 when they sang, "The Lord is my strength and my song; he has become my salvation."

He has declared that he will set you in praise [*tehillah*], fame, and honor high above all the nations he has made and that you will be a people holy unto the Lord your God as he promised (Deuteronomy 26:19).

Cry out, "Save us, O God our Saviour; gather us and deliver us from the nations, that we may give thanks to your holy name, that we may glory in your praise [*tehillah*]" (1 Chronicles 16:35).

As they began to sing [*rinnah*, which means "to shout a song"] and praise [*tehillah*], the Lord set ambushments against the men of Ammon and Moab and Mount Seir who were invading Judah, and they were defeated (2 Chronicles 20:22).

Stand up and praise [*barak*] the Lord your God, who is from everlasting to everlasting. Blessed be your glorious name, and may it be exalted above all blessing and praise [*tehillah*] (Nehemiah 9:5*b*).

For long ago, in the days of David and Asaph, there had been directors for the singers and for the songs of praise [*tehillah*]and thanksgiving to God (Nehemiah 12:46).

And provide for those who grieve in Zion–to bestow on them a crown of beauty instead of ashes, the oil of gladness instead of mourning, and a garment of praise [*tehillah*] instead of a spirit of despair (Isaiah 61:3).

For additional references, see Appendix E.

Zamar

This word is used almost exclusively in poetry. Its occurrences outside the Psalms are rare. It means "to pluck the strings of an instrument, to sing, to praise." It is a musical word and is largely involved with joyful expressions of music. It is used approximately forty times in expression of praise. (Only four of these are outside the Psalms). It is used in 1 Chronicles 16:9, one of the greatest chapters of praise in the entire Bible. "Sing to him, sing praise [*zamar*] to him; tell of all his wonderful acts." It is interesting that in this chapter there are four different Hebrew words translated "praise." In verse 35 it is *tehillah*. In verse 36, it is *barak* in the first part of the verse and *hallal* in the last part. How deep and varied are these expressions of praise!

For additional references, see Appendix E.

Todah

This word is used in connection with an offering and can be taken to mean "to extend the hands in a sacrifice of praise, thanksgiving, or thank-offering." In at least one case it seems to involve that which is not yet visible. It is an act of faith beyond which God moves to bring deliverance. This is seen in Psalm 50:23: "He who sacrifices thank-offerings [*todah*] honors me and he prepares the way so that I may show him the salvation of God." It may be at this point that the *sacrifice of praise* is most significant. Here in *todah* we have the type of praise that does not yet see the victory, the solution, or the answer. Common sense, human visibilities, and logic are sacrificed along with the "thank-offering" of *todah*.

It is both interesting and significant that this is the word used in Leviticus in connection with the offerings of thanksgiving. These references are to the *fellowship offering*.

These are the regulations for the fellowship offering a person may present to the Lord: If he offers it as an expression of thankfulness, then along with this sacrifice of thanksgiving [*todah*] he is to offer cakes of bread made without yeast and mixed with oil, wafers made without yeast and spread with oil, and cakes of fine flour well-kneaded and mixed with oil. Along with his fellowship offering of thanksgiving [*todah*] he is to present an offering with cakes of bread made with yeast. The meat of his fellowship offering of thanksgiving [*todah*] must be eaten on the day it is offered; he must leave none of it till morning (Leviticus 7:11-13,15).

Significant Usages of *Todah*

> These things I remember as I pour out my soul; how I used to go with the multitude, leading the procession to the house of God, with shouts of joy and thanksgiving [*todah*] among the festive throng (Psalm 42:4).

Sacrifice thank offerings [*todah*] to God, fulfill your vows to the Most High (Psalm 50:14).
I am under vows to you, O God; I will present my thank offerings [*todah*] to you (Psalm 56:12).
Let us come before him with thanksgiving [*todah*] and extol him with music and song (Psalm 95:2).

The title of the one hundredth Psalm is "A Psalm for Giving Thanks" [*todah*]. An interesting combination of Hebrew words for praise is given in Psalm 100:4: "Enter his gates with thanksgiving [*todah*] and his courts with praise [*tehillah*]; give thanks to him and praise [*barak*] his name."

This sequence is worthy of investigation. First there is thanksgiving offered, sometimes by sheer faith. For all of us there are times when this is the only place to begin genuine worship. The circumstances have not produced emotional reassurance. Visible hopes are diminished, but we start with thanksgiving by faith [*todah*]. Then, having come through the gate of thanksgiving, we stand in the court of praise with song [*tehillah*]. In the midst of continued thanksgiving we engage in blessing [*barak*] the Lord! Hallelujah!

Another interesting combination of Hebrew words is found in Psalm 147:7. "Sing [*zamar*] to the Lord with thanksgiving [*todah*]; make music to our God on the harp." What a pleasant realization that we are made for praise in such a manner that varying kinds of praise can be engaged in at the same time!

Do you remember our mention of praise preparing the way for miraculous deliverance? Fresh proof of this facet of praise is given in Jonah 2:9. "But I, with a song of thanksgiving [*todah*], will sacrifice to you. What I have vowed I will make good. Salvation comes from the Lord." The very next verse reported, "And the Lord commanded the fish and it vomited Jonah onto dry land."

Other references for *todah* are found in Appendix E.

Shabach

This word means "to shout, to address in a loud tone, to commend." It is the exclamatory form of praise. This particular word for "shout" is translated "praise" only a few times:

Because your love is better than life, my lips will glorify [*shabach*] you (Psalm 63:3). KJV: "My lips shall praise thee"

Praise [*hallal*] the Lord, all you nations; extol [*shabach*] him all you peoples (Psalm 117:1). KJV: "Praise him, all ye people"

One generation will commend [*shabach*] your works to another; they will tell of your might acts (Psalm 145:4). KJV: "One generation shall praise thy works..."

Extol [*shabach*] the Lord, O Jerusalem; praise [*hallal*] your God, O Zion (Psalm 147:12). KJV: "Praise the Lord, O Jerusalem"

The correspondent word to *shabach* is *shebach* and is used in connection with praise in three places in Daniel. On the first occasion Daniel testified, "I thank and praise [*shebach*] you, O God of my fathers; you have given me wisdom and power, you have made known to me what we asked of you, and you have made known to us the dream of the king" (2:23). The other two cases have to do with Nebuchadnezzar's restoration to sanity. "At the end of that time, I, Nebuchadnezzar, raised my eyes toward heaven, and my sanity was restored. Then I praised [KJV: "blessed," *barak*] the Most High; I honored [*shebach*] and glorified him who lives forever" (4:34). Further he testifies, "Now I, Nebuchadnezzar, praise [*shebach*] and exalt and glorify the King of heaven, because everything he does is right and all his ways are just. And those who walk in pride he is able to humble" (4:37).

Conclusion

Do not trip lightly over this material if you really want to delve into the depths of the meaning of praise. I hope you will find this chapter, the Appendices, and the following tables of word meanings of tremendous help in your personal study and practice of praise. I have covered only the seven principal words in the Hebrew language which are *translated* as "praise." There are many other words, though which *refer* to the act of praise. You will find them in the table on pages 90-91. Let us summarize the words we have covered here with the simplest statement of their meanings:

Hallal: "to laud, boast, rave, to celebrate"–It is used approximately one hundred times in the Old Testament.

Yadah: "to worship with extended hands, to throw out the hands–It is used over ninety times in the Old Testament. (*Yad* means "hand.")

Barak: "to bless, to declare God the origin of power for success, prosperity, and fertility." It is used approximately seventy times in the Old Testament as praise to God.

Tehillah: "to sing or laud"–It is derived from *hallal* and is generally accepted to mean "the singing of *hallals.*" It is used over fifty times in the Old Testament.

Zamar: "to pluck the strings of an instrument, to praise with song"–It is used almost exclusively in the Psalms and occurs approximately forty times in the Old Testament.

Todah: "to extend the hands in thanksgiving, a thank-offering"–It is used only a few times when translated "praise" but occurs many other times in connection with thanksgiving.

Shabach (*Shebach*): "to commend, address in a loud tone, to shout"–This is the exclamatory form of praise in a special sense and is found only about seven times in the Old Testament. It is interesting, however, to note that other words for "shout" are used in connection with the exercise of praise. (See the chart on other Hebrew word meanings).

Projects in Praise

1. Memorize the seven words we have studied in this chapter and their respective meanings with at least one scripture reference for each of them.
2. Begin to mark your Bible where there are references to praise, noting by the reference the Hebrew word used. (I have found this to be a most rewarding endeavor, time-consuming but valuable)

TABLE DENOTING HEBREW WORDS FOR PRAISE

Note: This table excludes those we have already discussed.

English Transliteration for the Hebrew Word	English Meaning	Times Used Relating to Praise
Gadal	magnify, praise	6
Gil	shout, circle in joy	29
Zakar	remember, acknowledge, praise	12
Zamir	song	4
Zimrah	song	6

Hadah	rejoice	1
Havah	worship, kneel, prostrate	65
Hul	dance	1
Haphetz	delight, take pleasure in	3
Hillul	celebration of thanksgiving	1
	(for harvest)	(Leviticus 19:24)
Yahav	give, ascribe	7
Kaved	honor, glorify	12
Karat	dance	2
Mizmor	psalm	57
Maha	clap	1
Mahol	dance (noun)	5
Meholah	dance (noun)	2
Neginah	music, song, string music	8
Nagan	play stringed instrument	2
Nasa	lift (voice)	4
Natan	proclaim, strike, give	4
Selal	exalt, sing	1
Saphar	recount, proclaim	18
Avar	let resound	1
Alaz	exult	6
Alatz	rejoice	5
Anah	testify (sing)	1
Paar	boast, glorify	1
Pazaz	leap	1
Patzah	burst forth with	6
Tzahal	shout for joy	1
Tzavah	cry aloud	1
Qara	proclaim, call out	1
Rum	exalt, extol	8
Rua	shout in triumph	13
Rinnah	shout of joy	18
Ranan	shout with joy	42
Renanah	shout of joy	2
Raqad	dance, skip about	1
Sus	rejoice	10
Sahaq	play, dance	4
Samah	rejoice, be glad	64
Shavah	glorify, praise	6
Shir	sing	31
Shama	proclaim	10

11 Praise: A Word Study in Greek

The Greek language has also made contributions to our understanding of praise. As in Hebrew where there are several words *translated* "praise" but many more *connected* with praise, so it is in the Greek. First, let's deal with those words which are commonly translated "praise" and observe their usage. We will observe them alphabetically.

Ainesis, Ainos, Aineo

The first two of these words are nouns, the last a verb, and all are related. They are words only used in praise to God. In the Septuagint (the first five books of the Old Testament in Greek) *aineo* corresponds to *hallal* and *yadah*, the most common of the Hebrew words for "praise." (It is translated "praise" in every usage in the King James Version.) I will simply list the usages (NIV) below:

> Suddenly a great company of the heavenly host appeared with the angel, praising [*aineo*] God...(Luke 2:13).
>
> The shepherds returned, glorifying and praising [*aineo*] God for all the things that they had heard and seen, which were just as they had been told (Luke 2:20).
>
> Immediately he received his sight and followed Jesus, praising God. When all the people saw it, they also praised [*ainos*] God (Luke 18:43).

It should be noted that in the last two verses another word is used which is commonly translated "glorify" or "praise." We will look at that word later on under a discussion of *doxazo*.

> "Do you hear what these children are saying?" they asked him. "Yes," replied Jesus, "have you never read, 'From the lips of children and infants you have ordained praise [*ainos*]'?" (Matthew 21:16)

When they came near the place where the road goes down the Mount of Olives, the whole crowd of disciples began joyfully to praise [*aineo*] God in loud voices for all the miracles they had seen (Luke 19:37).

And they stayed continually at the temple, praising [*aineo*] God (Luke 24:53).

They broke bread in their homes and ate together with glad and sincere hearts, praising [*aineo*] God and enjoying the favor of all the people (Acts 2:46*b*, 47*a*).

He jumped to his feet and began to walk. Then he went with them into the temple courts, walking and jumping, and praising [*aineo*] God. When all the people saw him walking and praising [*ainew*] God, they recognized him as the same man who used to sit begging... (Acts 3:8-10*a*)

...Praise [*aineo*] the Lord, all you Gentiles, and sing praises [*epaineo*] to him, all you peoples (Romans 15:11).

Through Jesus, therefore, let us continually offer to God a sacrifice of praise [*ainesis*]—the fruit of lips that confess his name (Hebrews 13:15).

Doxa (noun), *Doxazo* (verb)

The word *doxa* and its verb form *doxazo* are generally translated "glory" and "glorify" respectively. The New International Version sometimes translates it "praise" in both noun and verb form. It comes from a word meaning "to seem or to suppose." It signifies an opinion, an estimate, or an honor resulting from a good opinion. Whether translated "glory," "glorify," or "praise" it is a good word in ascribing to God the honor due Him. Let us look at some of the references in the New Testament.

Glory [*doxa*] to God in the highest and on earth peace to men on whom his favor rests (Luke 2:14).

Immediately he received his sight and followed Jesus, praising [*doxazo*] God. [Note: *ainos* is used in the next part of the verse, yet the word is translated "praise" in the NIV.] "When all the people saw it, they also praised [*ainos*] God (Luke 18:43)

It is interesting to observe that Herod was smitten with worms and died when he refused "to give praise [*doxa*] to God" (Acts 12:23).

Paul, in recounting Abraham's faith, said, "Yet he did not waver through unbelief regarding the promise of God, but was strengthened in his faith and gave glory [*doxa*] to God" (Romans 4:20).

Our word "doxology" is taken from the word *doxa.* One of the famous doxologies of the Bible is found in Romans 11:36. "For from him and through him and to him are all things. To him be glory [*doxa*] forever! Amen."

A common form of praise is sounded in Galatians 1:5, Philippians 4:20, 1 Peter 4:11, and 2 Peter 3:18 using the word *doxa.* All of these verses say in different words, 'To him be glory both now and forever! Amen.'

The following are all translated "praise" in The New International Version:

> In the same way, let your light shine before men, that they may see your good deeds and praise [*doxazo*] your Father in heaven (Matthew 5:16).
>
> When the crowd saw this, they were filled with awe; and they praised [*doxazo*] God who had given such authority to men (Matthew 9:8).
>
> The people were amazed when they saw the dumb speaking, the crippled made well, the lame walking, and the blind seeing. And they praised [*doxazo*] the God of Israel (Matthew 15:31).
>
> So that with one heart and mouth you may glorify [*doxazo*] the God and Father of our Lord Jesus Christ (Romans 15:6).

Note: In the next verse (v. 7) the word *doxa* is translated "praise" in the NIV. "Accept one another, then, just as Christ accepted you, in order to bring praise [*doxa*] to God."

Many other references to these words are made in the New Testament. The reader may wish to pursue this study with the aid of a good concordance. The concluding statement on *doxazo* in *Vine's Complete Expository Dictionary of Old and New Testament Words* is excellent:

> As the glory of God is the revelation and manifestation of all that He has and is …, it is said of a Self-revelation in which God manifests all the goodness that is His, John 12:28 ["Father, glorify {*doxazo*} Your name!"] So far as it is Christ through whom this is made manifest, He is said to glorify [*doxazo*] the Father, John 17:1,4; or the Father is glorified in Him, 13:31; 14:13; and Christ's meaning is analogous when He says to His disciples, 'Herein is My Father glorified, that ye bear much fruit; and so shall ye be My disciples,' John 15:8. When *doxazo* is predicated of Christ …, it means simply

> that His innate glory is brought to light, is made manifest..It is an act of God the Father in Him...As the revelation of the Holy Spirit is connected with the glorification of Christ, Christ says regarding Him, 'He shall glorify [*doxazo*] Me,' 16:14 (Cremer).

Added to the richness of the thought that we can bless the Lord is the transcendent realization that we can engage in an endeavor which results in God's glory, because His real innate character and worth are unveiled. This is the glory of praise! The act of praise unveils the riches of God both in character and content. Hallelujah!

Epainos (noun), *Epaineo* (verb)

The word for praise [*ainos*] is preceded by the preposition *epi* meaning "upon" which W. E. Vine indicates is a strengthened form of *ainos. Epainos* represents a turnaround in our study of praise in that it has to do with man's *being* praised instead of *speaking* praise. Kittel in his *Theological Dictionary of the New Testament* says of this word:

> The only value of *epainos* (approval, praise) is when it does not represent a general human judgment or popular evaluation but when it is the approval of man by God. In Ephesians and Philippians, *epainos* denotes the praise and worship of the community in its confession.

There are nine references in the New Testament which involve *epainos* relating to our study of praise. They are as follows:

> No, a man is a Jew if he is one inwardly; and circumcision is circumcision of the heart, by the Spirit, not by the written code. Such a man's praise [*epainos*] is not from men but from God (Romans 2:29).
>
> For rulers hold no terror for those who do right, but for those who do wrong. Do you want to be free from fear of the one in authority? Then do what is right and he will commend [*epainos*] you (Romans 13:3).
>
> Therefore judge nothing before the appointed time; wait till the Lord comes. He will bring to light what is hidden in darkness and will expose the motives of men's hearts. At that time each will receive his praise [*epainos*] from God (1 Corinthians 4:5).

In love he predestined us to be adopted as his sons through Jesus Christ, in accordance with his pleasure and will–to the praise [*epainos*] of his glorious grace, which he has freely given us in the One he loves (Ephesians 1:5-6).

In order that we, who were the first to hope in Christ, might be for the praise [*epainos*] of his glory (Ephesians 1:12).

Having believed, you were marked in him with a seal, the promised Holy Spirit, who is a deposit guaranteeing our inheritance until the redemption of those who are God's possession—to the praise [*epainos*] of his glory (Ephesians 1:13*b*-14).

Filled with the fruit of righteousness that comes through Jesus Christ—to the glory and praise [*epainos*] of God (Philippians 1:11).

Finally, brothers, whatever is true, whatever is noble, whatever is right, whatever is pure, whatever is lovely, whatever is admirable—if anything is excellent or praiseworthy [*epianos*]—think about such things (Philippians 4:8).

These have come so that your faith—of greater worth than gold, which perishes even though refined by fire—may be proved genuine and may result in praise [*epainos*], glory [*doxa*], and honor when Jesus Christ is revealed (1 Peter 1:7).

Note: There are also several references to praise using this word which relate to commendation between human beings. Our study, however, is of praise which relates to God or from God.

Eulogetos, Eulogia

This is a word that is never used of man, only of God. It means "blessed" or "praised." The word in the Hebrew that corresponds to this is *baruk* or *barak,* generally translated "blessed, blessing, or to bless." Zechariah, at the birth of his son, John the Baptist, was filled with the Spirit and began his first utterance with praise, saying, "Praise [*eulogetos*] be to the Lord, the God of Israel, because he has come and has redeemed his people" (Luke 1:68).

Our English word "eulogy" is a transliteration of the Greek word *eulogia.* The eulogy involves words of commendation and praise. Paul reminds us that God is ever being praised [*eulogetos*] (Romans 1:25; 9:5; and 2 Corinthians 11:31).

Other uses of these words are as follows:

Praise [*eulogetos*] be to the God and Father of our Lord Jesus Christ, the Father of compassion and the God of all comfort (2 Corinthians 1:3).

Praise [*eulogetos*] be to the God and Father of our Lord Jesus Christ, who has blessed us in the heavenly realms with every spiritual blessing in Christ (Ephesians 1:3).

Praise [*eulogetos*] be to the God and Father of our Lord Jesus Christ! In his great mercy he has given us new birth into a living hope through the resurrection of Jesus Christ from the dead (1 Peter 1:3).

Out of the same mouth come praise [*eulogia*] and cursing. My brothers, this should not be (James 3:10).

In a loud voice they sang: "Worthy is the Lamb who was slain, to receive power and wealth and wisdom and strength and honor and glory and praise [*eulogia*]!"(Revelation 5:12)

Then I heard every creature in heaven and on earth and under the earth and on the sea, and all that is in them, singing: "To him who sits on the throne and to the Lamb be praise [*eulogia*] and honor and glory and power, for ever and ever!" (Revelation 5:13)

… saying: "Amen! Praise [*eulogia*] and glory and wisdom and thanks and honor and power and strength be to our God for ever and ever. Amen!" (Revelation 7:12)

Again we realize that the glory of this word to us is that we are capable of blessing the Lord with words. Out of that God-given ability comes the joy of blessing others as well.

Exomologeomai

This is a derivative of *homologeo* which means "to confess." The preposition *ek* which means "out of" makes the word stronger and more intense. It may be taken to mean "to confess forth openly and freely." It is translated "praise" in the NIV at least three times, two of these referring to praise from the lips of Jesus. They are as follows:

At that time Jesus said, "I praise [*exomologeomai*] you, Father, Lord of heaven and earth because you have hidden these things from the wise and learned, and revealed them to little children" (Matthew 11:25).

At that time Jesus, full of joy through the Holy Spirit, said, "I praise [*exomologeomai*] you, Father, Lord of heaven and earth, because you have hidden these things from the wise and learned, and revealed them to little children. Yes, Father, for this was your good pleasure"(Luke 10:21).

Therefore I will praise [*exomologeomai*] you among the Gentiles..." (Romans 15:9*b)*.

Humneo, Humnos

This word simply means "to sing praise." Only one time is it translated "praise." That is in Hebrews 2:12: "I will declare your name to my brothers; in the presence of the congregation I will sing your praises [*humneo*]. The Greek Interlinear simply states: "I will hymn you." Other uses are: Matthew 26:30; Mark 14:26; Acts 16:25; Ephesians 5:19; and Colossians 3:16.

There is another reference to praise I want to mention here. "But you are a chosen people, a royal priesthood, a holy nation, a people belonging to God, that you may *declare the praises* of him who called you out of darkness into his wonderful light"(1 Peter 2:9). The phrase in italics, *declare the praises*, uses two Greek words. The first is *exangelo* which means "to proclaim or to put out a message." (*Angelos* is used with reference to angels or messengers.) The other word is *arate* which means "virtue or praise."

Megaluno

This word means "to make great, large, or long or to magnify." The NIV renders this word "praise" in two instances. In Luke 1:46 Mary's song begins with these words, "My soul praises [*megaluno*] the Lord and my spirit rejoices in God my Savior." It is also used when Peter was at the house of Cornelius and the Spirit was poured out upon the Gentiles: "For they heard them speaking in tongues and praising [*megaluno*] God" (Acts 10:46).

The same word is used in Acts 19:17 but is translated differently in the NIV. When the sons of Sceva tried unsuccessfully to cast out demons, the news traveled rapidly: "When this became known to the Jews and Greeks living in Ephesus, they were all seized with fear, and the name of the Lord Jesus was held in high honor [*megaluno*]." Though it has been translated differently, the Greek word is the same. Praise is the definite connotation. It is worthy of mention that this word *megaluno* is the word which corresponds to the Hebrew word *gadal* which means "to extol."

Psallo (verb), *Psalmos* (noun)

This word means "to sing praise in spiritual ecstasy or to make melody." For our study the most significant fact about this word is that in the Septuagint it is the Greek rendering of the word *zamar*, meaning "to sing or to pluck the strings of an instrument" and is used some forty times. It is also used ten times for the Hebrew word *ranan*, meaning "to shout for joy." The noun *psalmos* simply means a song of praise.

The four uses in the New Testament are as follows:

> So that the Gentiles may glorify [*doxazo*] God for his mercy, as it is written: "Therefore I will praise [*exomologeomai*] you among the Gentiles; I will sing hymns [*psallo*] to your name" (Romans 15:9).
>
> So what shall I do? I will pray with my spirit, but I will also pray with my mind; I will sing [*psallo*] with my spirit, but I will also sing [*psallo*] with my mind (1 Corinthians 14:15).
>
> Speak to one another with psalms [*psalmos*], hymns and spiritual songs. Sing and make music [*psallo*] in your heart to the Lord (Ephesians 5:19).
>
> Is any one of you in trouble? He should pray. Is anyone happy? Let him sing songs of praise [*psallo*] (James 5:13). This is the only place where it is translated "songs of praise."

Other Words Denoting Praise but Not So Translated

As in the chapter on Hebrew word study, I have gone into detail only on words which are *translated* in the NIV as "praise." The table below shows other words not yet mentioned.

TABLE DENOTING GREEK WORDS FOR PRAISE

English Transliteration for the Greek Word	English Meaning	Times Used Relating to Praise
Agallio	exult, be glad	10
Ado	sing	2
Allomai	leap	1
Anthomologeomai	praise, thank	1
Gonupeteo	kneel down	4

Euphraino	rejoice	5
Eucharisteo	give thanks	35
Eucharistia	thanksgiving	14
Eucharastos	thankful	1
Kampto	to bend the knee	2
Kauchaomai	to boast	8
Pipto	to fall to the ground	15
Proskuneo	to fall down and worship	42
Skirtao	to leap with joy	3
Sunadomai	to rejoice	1
Chairo	to rejoice	28
Charis	thanks, grace	7
Oda	song	5
Hosanna	save, Lord	5

Note: You will notice that I have not mentioned a very important word for praise in the New Testament—hallelujah. This is because it was covered in a previous chapter. It is simply a translation of the Hebrew word by the same pronunciation, which means "praise Jehovah."

Projects in Praise

1. Memorize at least three of the major Greek words for praise in the New Testament and at least one instance of each word's usage.
2. Memorize 1 Timothy 1:17 which reads, "Now to the King eternal, immortal, invisible, the only God, be honor and glory for ever and ever. Amen."
3. Mark other references to praise in your New Testament. You will find many surrounding the birth of Jesus. (We will be studying these later.) You will also find many others in Revelation.
4. Review your previous memory verses, especially Psalm 119:164.
5. Determine to carry out the stated intentions of that verse and praise the Lord at least seven times a day. Remember to praise the Lord upon awakening, retiring, eating (three times), during a morning *praise break* and an afternoon *praise break*.

12 People Protesting Praise

Praise is not without its adversaries. The devil despises it and will do all within his power to quiet it. Unregenerate human logic finds the practice of praise enigmatic and will seek to suggest something more sensible. Carnality finds it threatening and intimidating and will tempt people to crush the practice of praise where possible.

The recovery of praise for the body of Christ may be fiercely contested. We should understand this first so when opposition arises we will not be caught in reactionary tactics. If praise is right we need not defend the exercise of it. Neither do we need to counterattack those who fight it. I have been receiving calls from churches where Biblical praise is beginning to be practiced. The first result is a reaction that praise is new, revolutionary, and smacks of fanaticism. That reaction generally comes from some within the heart of the leadership, who, for the most part, are well-intentioned and genuinely concerned about the general welfare of the church. What happens next is largely up to the pastor and church staff. *If* there is defense and counterattack, the plot thickens and the congregation polarizes, resulting in division and confusion and rejection.

Consequently, the principal reason for this chapter is to sound a caution as well as a challenge. The caution is against expecting an immediate and unanimous positive response from any congregation of people. The challenge is to plot a course of deliberate, scriptural education relating to the principles and practice of praise—steering the course with guarded zeal.

First, I will deal with some scriptural examples of people who protested praise. They probably have unwitting kinfolk in our midst today. I would not leave the impression that all who protest praise in any measure are filled with evil intentions. This would be an unfair and oversimplified observation. It is a valid consideration, though, as we measure the response to praise throughout history. We will first observe the people who protested praise and the results of this protest in their lives.

Michal

Michal was David's wife and the daughter of Saul. This story centers around her response to the praises of her husband, King David, and his exercise of exciting praise. (See 1 Chronicles 13-15.) Saul and Jonathan had died and David had been confirmed as king. One of his first executive decisions as king was to return the ark of the covenant to its rightful place in the capital. The ark was significant to the spiritual life of the nation because it was emblematic of the presence of God among His people, and it kept them reminded of their covenant relationship with Him.

The first attempt was ill-fated when the ark was placed on a newly constructed cart instead of upon the shoulders of divinely appointed men. The result was the death of a man named Uzzah, with the subsequent decision of David to detour the ark to the house of Obed-Edom. It was a case of "right mission and wrong manner." It was right to bring the ark back, but the method used should have been carefully sought out from God. Ultimately, the task was carried out in the right manner, and the ark was transported to the City of David with the sounding of rams' horns, trumpets, cymbals, lyres, and harps.

The sight of the returning ark, with all it represented, the regal entourage accompanying it, and the service of worship and sacrifice which accompanied its return were more than the delighted heart of David could contain. He simply went into a "holy dance." In 1 Chronicles he is described as *dancing and celebrating* ("playing" in the KJV). The Hebrew word used here for *dance* is one which means "to stamp, jump, leap, spring about wildly, or skip." In the corresponding passage (2 Samuel 6:16), the description involves the words *dancing* and *leaping*. David's spontaneous exercise of praise was unrehearsed and wholehearted.

As Michal watched the proceedings from a window, she saw David leaping, dancing, and doubtlessly singing—and "she despised him in her heart." The confrontation between Michal and David is recorded in 2 Samuel 6:20-22. It is impossible to know all that prompted Michal to respond as she did, but certain conclusions can be drawn from the text. When David returned home to bless his family, Michal was waiting. The anger and offense in her heart erupted as she came out to meet him. She rebuked him with, "How the king of Israel has distinguished himself today, disrobing in the sight of the slave girls of his servants as any vulgar fellow would!"

There are two implications here which could provide insight into the reasons for her bitter offense. First, it appears that her sense of dignity had been violated. David had not acted in a manner in which she thought a king should act. When she saw him praise, her image of kingly behavior—as she had learned to view it—was out of order. She could not cope with the sudden change in her husband's deportment. Anger and bitterness resulted and occasioned this malignant accusation.

The second reason is implied in the mention of the slave girls. He had done what his excitement and pleasure had dictated with no thought of who was around. This is the spirit of genuine praise. It is oblivious to its surroundings, not caring who is watching. Michal did not share in the excitement. She simply did not grasp the meaning and significance of the event; she was more sensitive about what the slave girls saw when the king was dancing. In her outburst she may have revealed a root of jealousy. That her response was sinful is implied in verse 23: she was barren.

In the final analysis we can only speculate as to the *reasons* for her opposition to praise. Clearly, she had no appreciation for the spiritual implications of that great hour. Perhaps the same root problem exists today. Those who have not seen God in their hearts are bound to have differing evaluations from those who have. Their reactions will reflect their true feelings but should not deter us from the determination to praise the Lord.

David's response comes in the spirit we should all have:

> It was before the Lord, who chose me rather than your father or anyone from his house when he appointed me ruler over the Lord's people Israel–I will celebrate before the Lord. I will become even more undignified than this, and I will be humiliated in my own eyes. But by these slave girls you spoke of, I will be held in honor (vv.21, 22).

Undaunted by the reproach of his wife, David answered in effect, "You haven't seen anything yet. At all costs I will celebrate before the Lord!" Amen! Amen!

Athaliah

Athaliah was a wicked queen who murdered without hesitation to protect her position. She never should have been queen. Upon the death of her son Ahaziah, she had ordered all the princes murdered and seized the throne for herself for six years. However, Joash, the son of Ahaziah and rightful heir to the throne, was hidden away at the Temple of the Lord.

After six years of corruption and injustice under Athaliah, Jehoiada the priest called together the commanders of the battalions, entered into covenant with them, and planned the coronation of Joash, the rightful king. (See 2 Kings 11.) Jehoiada gave Joash a copy of the covenant and then proclaimed Joash the King of Judah. The people began to clap their hands and shout, "Long live the king!" When Athaliah heard the noise of their acclamation she ran to the Temple of the Lord. As she entered the Temple, she saw the people rejoicing and blowing the trumpets in glad celebration, and she knew the praises of the people sounded a death knell to her unjust reign. Jehoiada then made a covenant between the Lord and the king and the people that they would be the Lord's people. Revival resulted, the temple of Baal was torn down, the idols to Baal smashed, and the priest of Baal was killed in front of the heathen altars.

Athaliah protested praise because she knew that praise and injustice could not long dwell together. One would cancel the other in a short time. Praise will always arouse insecurity where there is unjust authority; therefore, praise will also meet its fiercest detractors among those whose positions are thus threatened by its exercise.

Job's Wife

Job's wife also protested praise. Job had suffered the loss of his possessions as well as his children. After these crushing blows his response was, "Naked I came from my mother's womb, and naked I will depart. The Lord gave and the Lord has taken away; may the name of the Lord be praised" (Job 1:21). This was Job's determination even though he lost his most-treasured personal possession, his health. But his wife chided, "Are you still holding on to your integrity? Curse God and die!" In other words, "Stop praising God and start cursing God!" Job's response was immediate, "You are talking like a foolish woman. Shall we accept good from God, and not trouble?" (Job 2:9-10).

He was approved for his determination to praise: "In all this, Job did not sin in what he said" (Job 2:10*b*).

Job's wife had problems which caused her to protest praise: ignorance and shortsightedness. She could not see beyond the immediate circumstances to the sovereignty of a loving God.

The Pharisees

The Pharisees protested praise wherever it was sounded. When Jesus made His triumphal entry into Jerusalem, the crowds shouted, "Hosanna to the Son of David! Blessed is he who comes in the name of the Lord!" (Matthew 21:9) He went into the Temple and overturned the tables of the moneychangers and dove sellers. He healed the lame and the blind amid shouts of praise from the children. The chief priests and the teachers of the law asked indignantly, "Do you hear what these children are saying?" They hated praise because they hated Jesus. They hated Jesus because He did not fit into their religious identity. He wrecked their man-made systems and crippled their ceremonies. The very sound of praise set their teeth on edge. Christless religionists always protest praise.

It would be wise for us to consider the company one may join when praise is opposed. Not only are there people who protest praise, but certain problems sometimes prevail to prohibit praise.

Hidden Sins

Unconfessed sin in the life of the believer restricts praise. Therefore, repentance—complete and thorough—is a necessity to unhindered praise. A law relating to revival and praise is stated in Proverbs 28:13: "He who conceals his sins does not prosper, but whoever confesses and renounces them finds mercy." Remember that the brazen laver had to be passed before entrance to the Holy Place of the Tabernacle. At that laver the priests were told to wash their hands and feet "that they [would] not die" (Exodus 30:21). Cleansing was to precede worship. That is still true today. We need not do penance or make sacrifices; the debt has already been paid, but we must be cleansed from any hindrance of sin in our lives. The psalmist wrote, "Bless the Lord, O my soul: and all that is within me, bless his holy name" (Psalm 103:1, KJV). That great declaration presupposes total cleansing from sin. If sin is in the praiser, he or she cannot bless the Lord because ***praise involves "all that is within us."***

We are guilty of concealing sin if we stop short of God's prescribed method for dealing with it. We may rationalize, compensate, deny, or disregard, but none of these will suffice. We must submit to God's proposition. "If we confess our sins, he is faithful and just and will forgive us our sins and purify us from all unrighteousness" (1 John 1:9).

The psalmist declared, "If I had cherished sin in my heart, the Lord would not have listened" (Psalm 66:18). Sin unconfessed in the heart of the would-be praiser stifles the sound of praise and may even produce the guilt which paralyzes praise.

Paul gave young Timothy sound advice: "Flee the evil desires of youth, and pursue righteousness, faith, love and peace, along with those who call on the Lord out of a pure heart" (2 Timothy 2:22).

If there is an inner resistance to praise, we had best look for unconfessed sin.

Ignorance

The church today is largely illiterate regarding the subject of praise. A friend of mine once commented, "Folks are generally *down* on what they are not *up* on!" Regarding praise, that statement was never truer than it is now. Misunderstanding abounds because of ignorance.

I was ignorant regarding praise in both its content and its intent. My mind exploded when I began to see its centrality in the history of God's revelation of Himself to the world. A cursory investigation of the Scriptures on the subject will be shocking to most folks. The praise issue is not marginal or peripheral—it is central!

I have never appreciated the word of Jesus relating to freedom and the knowledge of the truth more than I do now. "Then you will know the truth, and the truth will set you free" (John 8:32). I have happily discovered that genuine believers always respond to the truth; as they do, it makes them free. If there is not freedom in an area of life, it is because the truth has not been received and allowed to do its work in that area. As an individual accepts the truth about praise, freedom regarding praise always develops. When a congregation begins to **accept** the Biblical truth about praise, there begins to be freedom in their corporate exercise of praise.

I would urge the pastors and staff to educate their people

about praise: what it is, why it is, its vast potential. Deliberately lead in its exercise. Don't curse the darkness; light a lamp. Don't mourn the ignorance; teach the truth.

Pride

Nothing strikes a blow at pride like praise. David remarked to Michal, "I will become even more undignified than this, and I will be humiliated in my own eyes" (2 Samuel 6:22). Michal's sense of dignity (and often our dignity is false and humanistic) had been offended. David's choices were to capitulate and accommodate her offense or to go on in praise.

Most congregations possess several forms of pride. Many of us have experienced all of them.

- There is the pride involved in fearing to lose face in the eyes of others. We feel we have an image to protect, and many of our actions are weighed in the light of their effect on our image.
- Then there is the pride of race. This is rooted in the feeling that the color of a man's skin causes his net worth to appreciate or depreciate. Until I am able to worship freely with anyone, regardless of race, my praise will be hindered.
- There is pride of place. If I have a feeling of elevation because of my social status, financial worth, or peer recognition, praise will be stifled.
- Perhaps the most subtle of all is "grace-pride." This sort of pride eases in on the supposition that the magnitude of God's blessings on my life indicate a superiority of spirituality on my part. It must be remembered that Uzziah of old was mightily blessed of the Lord as long as he sought God: "...he was greatly helped until he became powerful. But after Uzziah became powerful, his pride led to his downfall" (2 Chronicles 26:15*b*-16). Sounds of praise died out under the clamorous noise of pride. Unfaithfulness was the next step and devastation the result.

Praise will serve to expose every form of pride for what it is because pride is unmasked by genuine, Biblical praise. Either pride will stop the progress of praise or praise will root up and destroy pride.

Tradition

Let me speak first on behalf of tradition, since it has few friends today. There is a spirit abroad that dictates the destruction of tradition without question, but when we really think about it, the only forms which deserve to become traditions are those which have proven workable, credible, and profitable. Good traditions should be preserved at any cost, but some traditions—like the baby's bath water—need to be respectfully discarded when their usefulness has been served. I wish to speak about those here.

I have become convinced that in every community and church there have grown actual strongholds and curses of tradition. As strange as it may sound to many a religious ear, I further believe that there are hordes of demons who are specialists in preserving worthless and damaging traditions. The result is that many well-meaning believers protest Bible truth and Biblical practices in the name of "defending the faith"—when, in fact, they are guarding meaningless traditions which should have been discarded long ago.

It is frequently difficult to distinguish between conviction and taste (based on tradition). But the distinction is necessary or else we will find ourselves somewhere down the line opposing God Himself!

Another warning must be sounded here. Dynamiting unwanted traditions often causes unprofitable damage in other areas. The best method of dealing with such traditions involves the introduction of Biblical concepts instead.

Projects in Praise

1. Take time to read the episodes involving Michal (2 Chronicles 13-15), Athaliah (2 Kings 11), and Job's wife (Job 2).
2. Put yourself in their places and see if you can detect any of their feelings in you.
3. List any feelings of protest you have felt toward the personal or corporate exercise of praise. Trace these feelings honestly to their source and acknowledge them before God.
4. Review your memory work, especially your daily determination to praise (Psalm 113:3; 119:164; 150:6).
5. Determine today that you will rejoice and be glad. Quote Psalm 118:24, "This is the day the Lord has made; let us [me] rejoice and be glad in it."
6. Memorize and quote through the next days, "For the joy of the Lord is your [my] strength" (Nehemiah 8:10).

13 People Who Praise the Lord

"She conceived again, and when she gave birth to a son she said, 'This time I will praise the Lord.' So she named him Judah" (Genesis 29:35).

The Scripture records the stories of many people who praised God. We can all give praisers the collective name of the tribe of Judah, however, because of the following account.

Jacob had worked for Laban, and Laban's daughter Rachel was to be the reward of that lengthy labor. But his reward—because of Laban's trickery—was Leah, Rachel's weak-eyed sister. One can imagine Jacob's disappointment as he awakened after his wedding night to realize that the *wrong* woman was his wife. As he worked seven more years for the hand of Rachel in marriage, several children were born to him by Leah. The first was Reuben, of whom Leah declared, "It is because the Lord has seen my misery. Surely my husband will love me now." The second son was Simeon of whom she observed, "Because the Lord heard that I am not loved, he gave me this one too." The third was Levi, at whose birth she stated, "Now at last my husband will become attached to me, because I have borne him three sons." (See Genesis 29:32-35.)

In the names of her first three children by Jacob, there is a crying out to be loved, to have a sense of belonging; but her relationship remained technical, legal, and cold with Jacob. What happened between the third and fourth child is not clear. It's possible that either Leah felt that the child she was carrying was conceived in love, and that her marriage was at last a relationship of warmth and vitality, or she gave her expectations to the Lord and stopped looking to her husband for acceptance. Whichever the case, she simply decided to praise the Lord and revealed that determination in the name of her fourth child. She called him *Judah*, which means "praise." It was then that joy came into her life as her son lived out the meaning of his name.

When Jacob lay dying, he spoke concerning each of his sons in a prophetic manner. Of Judah he said the following:

> Judah, your brothers will praise you; your hand will be on the neck of your enemies; your father's sons will bow down to you. You are a lion's cub, O Judah; you return from the prey, my son. Like a lion he crouches and lies down, like a lioness— who dares to rouse him? The scepter will not depart from Judah, nor the ruler's staff from between his feet, until he comes to whom it belongs and the obedience of the nations is his (Genesis 49:8,9).

What a glorious prophecy! No tribe will have as rich a destiny as this tribe called *praise*. The prophecy continues through verse 11, and the last statement in Jacob's prophecy refers to the coming of Jesus through the tribe of Judah (Genesis 49:10). The ultimate blessing of the tribe of Judah was that the Messiah was born into that tribe. It has always interested me that He was born to the tribe of praise and not to the priestly tribe of Levi. Christ's heritage is praise. When Christ lives in us, praise lives in us.

The results of the practice of praise are fairly standard throughout history. As the tribe of Judah lived consistently with its name, the results were glorious. With this history in mind let us observe some truths about all people who praise the Lord. It will help us to be more determined in our choice to praise and further aid us in understanding the benefits accruing to the exercise of praise.

People Who Praise Enjoy Prominence

People who praise are *praised!* After all, "Give, and it will be given to you," is an axiom which works in any realm (Luke 6:38*a*). As Jacob, obviously under the anointing of God, looked into Judah's future, he saw his other sons bowing down to Judah. Praise brings prominence! Praise glorifies God, and God exalts the praiser.

When people praise the Lord, there is reflected in them a character which causes others to depend on them for leadership. It was so with Judah; it will be so with us. As you read this chapter, also read the prophecy of Jacob in Genesis 49:8-10.

The prominence brought about by praise will be more than local. Enemies will be overcome by the power of praise. "Like a lion he crouches and lies down, like a lioness—who dares to rouse him?" (Genesis 49:9).

People who praise prevail consistently. What was true of Judah will apply to anyone who determines to praise: "The scepter will not depart from Judah, nor the ruler's staff from between his feet" (Genesis 49:10*a*).

I have never personally known anyone engaged in habitual praise to be overcome by bitterness, anxiety, resentment, and depression. Whether life will be lived in terror or trust will be determined by whether or not we choose to praise the Lord. In a real sense all the prophecies of Jacob for Judah belong to all who have received kinship with Jesus Christ, "the Lion from the tribe of Judah."

People Who Praise Are Best Prepared for Worship

> The Lord said to Moses and Aaron: "The Israelites are to camp around the Tent of Meeting some distance from it, each man under his standard with the banners of his family." On the east, toward the sunrise, the divisions of the camp of Judah are to encamp under their standard (Numbers 2:1-2).

With signal significance the camp of "praise" (Judah's tribe) was located closest to the entrance of the Tabernacle courtyard. Judah was located on the east side, the first tribe to see the rising of the sun.

People who praise the Lord live nearest the delights of true worship and are the first to view the dawn of hope to end the nights of dark despair. It is never very far from praise to deliverance. Praise parks us within sight of the gate of worship and consistently leads us into that experience.

Remember that Jehoshaphat was the king of the tribe called "praise." As long as the tribe was held to the Lord only, they greatly prospered. Under good King Jehoshaphat, massive armies were recruited and fortified cities were built. Wealth and honor surrounded the king. Jehoshaphat removed the high places of heathen worship and refused to consult the prophets of Baal. He sought the Lord and had the Book of the Law taught all over the land. From the tribe of Judah itself, all the commanders of the armies were recruited, one thousand in all. Also from the tribe of Judah were 780,000 fighting men. Benjamin's tribe provided 380,000 fighting men with bows and shields, ready for battle.

After the description of Judah's greatness, there is the sad record of an alliance with Ahab by marriage. When praise is mixed with compromise, trouble begins. In an ensuing battle, which Judah should never have entered, Ahab was killed. Upon Jehoshaphat's return to the palace, he was met with a stern reproach from the prophet Jehu. "Should you help the wicked and love those who hate the Lord? Because of this, the wrath of the Lord is upon you. There is, however, some good in you, for you have rid the land of the Asherah poles and have set your heart on seeking God" (2 Chronicles 19:2-3). Despite the fact that he had made a serious mistake in judgement, his willingness to seek the Lord with praise would keep the hand of God upon him. The evidence of this is obvious in the next chapter where the episode of miraculous deliverane is recorded. (See 2 Chronicles 20.)

People Who Praise Have Best Access to the Blessings of God

When Moses blessed the tribes as recorded in Deuteronomy 33, he said of Judah, "...Hear, O Lord, the cry of Judah; bring him to his people. With his own hands he defends his cause. Oh, be his help against his foes!" (v. 7). The practice of praise is the preface to answered prayer. Remember, Judah means "praise." Let's paraphrase this verse, substituting the word *praise* for *Judah*: "Hear, O Lord, the cry of praise; with his own hands praise defends his cause. Oh, be praise's help against praise's foes!" Can you appreciate the blessings implied?

First, there is answered prayer. Praise breaks through in prayer. When all other kinds of prayer seem to no avail, praise puts us over! This is due to the reality of the spiritual realm. More is accomplished than our eyes can see.

Second, the family is united. "Bring him to his people," Moses says in intercession for Judah. Our innumerable differences defy unity at the human level, but praise will draw us together! It will be the common gathering ground of all people in the assembly of the redeemed around the throne of God. As we become one with the Lion of the tribe of praise, we will find ourselves in spiritual unity with all others who name his name!

Third, there will be strength. "With his own hands he defends his cause," proclaims Moses. We have already observed how many times praise and strength are found together in the Scriptures. Recall the passage in Psalm 8:2 which says, "Out of the mouth of babes and sucklings hast thou ordained *strength* ..." (KJV) The King James Version also translates Matthew 21:16, "Out of the mouth of babes and sucklings hast thou perfected *praise* ..." (KJV). Strength and praise are one and the same!

Fourth, there is protection for the praiser. Moses petitions, "Be his help against his foes!" No wall is as mighty a defense as the exercise of praise. The most impregnable defense against the foes of the church is a wall of praise.

People Who Praise Continue as Conquerors

The opening words of the Book of Judges are revealing. The Israelites asked the Lord, "Who will be the first to go up and fight for us against the Canaanites?" The Lord immediately answered, "Judah [praise] is to go; I have given the land into their hands." It was the tribe of praise to whom God had granted the victory! And thus Judges 1 records their advance, attack, and victory over the Canaanites.

In the midst of the chapter (v. 19) we read, "The Lord was with the men of Judah [praise]. They took possession of the hill country, but they were unable to drive the people from the plains, because they had iron chariots." When praise retreats, the enemy becomes bold. Judges 1 reveals that though Judah overcame the Canaanites and pressed them into forced labor, the tribe did not drive them out completely. As long as they acted in accord with their name, they conquered. The moment of mixture was the moment of weakness, and to this day, that weakness has plagued Israel.

An interesting sidelight in this chapter may prove to be of tremendous import. In retrospect, verse 20 reads, "As Moses had promised, Hebron was given to Caleb, who drove from it the three sons of Anak." Caleb was the representative from the tribe of Judah [praise] who joined eleven others to spy out the land of Canaan. He and Joshua were the only ones who brought back a report which included faith in God. They were the only two of their generation who survived the forty years in the wilderness. Then, when under Joshua's leadership they entered the land, Caleb testified:

> You know what the Lord said to Moses the man of God at Kadesh Barnea about you [Joshua] and me [Caleb]. I was forty years old when Moses the servant of the Lord sent me from Kadesh Barnea to explore the land. And I brought him back a report according to my convictions, but my brothers who went up with me made the hearts of the people melt with fear. I, however, followed the Lord my God wholeheartedly. So on that day Moses swore to me, "The land on which your feet have walked will be your inheritance and that of your children forever, because you have followed the Lord my God whole-heartedly." Now then, just as the Lord promised, he has kept me alive for forty-five years since the time he said this to Moses, while Israel moved about in the desert. So here I am today, eighty-five years old! I am still as strong today as the day Moses sent me out; I'm just as vigorous to go out to battle now as I was then. Now give me this hill country that the Lord promised me that day. You yourself heard then that the Anakites were there and their cities were large and fortified, but, the Lord helping me, I will drive them out just as he said (Joshua 14:6-12).

Read that statement again and you will have observed the essence of the philosophy of a true praiser! Let's summarize the characteristics of a praising conqueror:

- First, he follows the Lord wholeheartedly (v. 8).
- Second, he is kept alive to enjoy the Lord's blessings (verse 10).
- Third, his strength and vigor are preserved (verse 11).
- Fourth, he anticipates the highest blessings and refuses to settle for anything less (verse 12).
- Fifth, he presupposes the faithfulness of God to keep His promises and proceeds accordingly (verse 12).
- Sixth, he overcomes the enemy and possesses the land as revealed in history.

Caleb, of the tribe of praise, proved to be an able representative of his heritage.

People Who Praise Best Reflect Their Reigning Lord

The history of praise is the history of God's mighty hand at work in the lives of mankind. Victory has always accompanied praise. It always will. The people who determine to praise will not only find promotion from the Lord and will be exalted in their city, they will joyfully see the release of God's power accomplishing His will.

The Representative of the People Who Praise (The Lion-Lamb)

Revelation 5 contains an intriguing paradox of the Lion and the Lamb. John saw a scroll sealed with seven seals. A mighty angel cried with a loud voice, "Who is worthy to break the seals and open the scroll?" But no one in earth and heaven was worthy. John wept and wept because no one was found. Then one of the elders said to John, "Do not weep! See, the Lion of the tribe of Judah [praise], the Root of David, has triumphed. He is able to open the scroll and its seven seals."

At this point John saw a Lamb who took the scroll from the hand of God. Then the twenty-four elders fell down before the Lamb and began to sing a new song. Angels, "numbering thousands upon thousands, and ten thousand times ten thousand," circled the throne, the elders, and the living creatures, singing, "Worthy is the Lamb, who was slain, to receive power and wealth and wisdom and strength and honor and glory and praise!" (Revelation 5:12). Then every creature in heaven and earth and sea joined in, singing, "To him who sits on the throne and to the Lamb be praise and honor and glory and power, for ever and ever!"

The Lion-Lamb, our Lord Jesus, is at the center of this praising multitude! What a combination in those two animals! One is fierce, the other peaceful. One is aggressive, the other passive. One is mighty, the other vulnerable. But in those combinations of qualities are the abilities to sense deeply, care greatly, and fight ably. On the one hand Judah's Lion steps forward with a record of total triumph. On the other, heaven's Lamb receives the scroll and unfolds God's redemptive plan. The Lion is a Lamb and the Lamb is a Lion. This is the spirit and disposition of praise. When it stands facing the enemy it is lion-like, but when it is confronted with deep human need, its lamb-like compassion and calmness are in order. People who praise reflect these qualities.

As we study the history of Judah right on through the story of Jesus, we become aware that as we joined Jesus, we joined the tribe called praise. Praise is in our roots, our heritage. Our banner, our name is Praise. And the Lion-Lamb is our leader!

Projects in Praise

1. Check a concordance to see how many times *Judah* is found in the Old Testament.
2. Find interesting references which might reflect characteristics of *praise*, the true name.
3. Exercise the privilege of praise with thanksgiving, that through faith in Jesus you have been added to the tribe of praise.
4. Find others who came from the tribe of Judah (David, Solomon, Asa, Jehoshaphat, Josiah, and so forth).
5. Look back to previous memory verses and rehearse them.

14 The Psychology of Praise

And those who walk in pride he is able to humble (Daniel 4:37*b*).

There is an arresting story in the Book of Daniel which revolves around the subject of praise. Daniel was so committed to God that his life centered around unconditional praise. He was not completely alone in this. There were four men—Shadrach, Meshach, Abednego, and Belteshazzar (Daniel)—who were true to God. From the beginning, they refused to defile themselves with the king's meat. They chose instead to eat a simple vegetarian diet and walk with their God. Their faithfulness was rewarded by key civil service jobs in the government of Babylonia. While they play an important role in our story, we will focus on the king they so powerfully influenced.

Nebuchadnezzar was one of the greatest kings of the East. His kingdom was mighty, and he was an able and powerful ruler. He was, in fact, selected by God to capture Jehoiakim, king of Judah, and to lead the nation of Judah captive. We are told in Daniel 1:2, "And the Lord delivered Jehoiakim king of Judah into his [Nebuchadnezzar's] hand..." In other words Nebuchadnezzar had done what he did by divine mandate. What a view of history! God is God over the nations of the world. He appoints their times and places. He is sovereign! Russia is where it is by God's plan, as are China, Arabia, and all the nations of the world.

We will look at three points of interest and significance.

First, the Effect of Praise on a Heathen Kingdom

Here were four men whose only objective in life was to glorify the God of heaven. Their faithfulness in minor things, such as diet and devotional exercises, brought them advancement and greatness. They requested and won the right to have the diet of their own choosing and proved that their appearance and energy level were superior to those of the servants who feasted on the king's fare. The report was, "At the end of the ten days they looked healthier and better nourished than any of the young men who ate the royal food" (Daniel 1:15). Thus they entered the king's service.

When heathen King Nebuchadnezzar had a dream beyond the ability of the magicians of the palace to interpret, the king was so enraged that he ordered the execution of all the wise men of Babylon—including Daniel and his friends, Shadrach, Meshach, and Abednego. They went before their God to plead for mercy. During the night Daniel received in a vision the meaning of the king's dream.

> Then Daniel praised the God of heaven and said: "Praise be to the name of God for ever and ever; wisdom and power are his. He changes times and seasons; he sets up kings and deposes them. He gives wisdom to the wise and knowledge to the discerning. He reveals deep and hidden things; he knows what lies in darkness, and light dwells with him. I thank and praise you, O God of my fathers: you have given me wisdom and power, you have made known to me what we asked of you, you have made known to us the dream of the king" (Daniel 2:19*b*-23).

There are few passages on praise in the entire Bible that parallel the transcendence of this one: their faithfulness and praise had opened mysteries.

The king was informed of Daniel's interpretation. Daniel was careful that all praise and glory went to God as he said, "There is a God in heaven who reveals mysteries..." (Daniel 2:28). Still later he said, "The God of heaven has given you dominion and power and might and glory" (Daniel 2:37*b*). Again he reported, "The great God has shown the king what will take place in the future.." (Daniel 2:45*b*). The faithfulness and praise of Daniel and his friends brought promotion. Upon having his dream interpreted, Nebuchadnezzar promoted them all—Daniel to a high office at the royal court and the other three to administrative positions over the provinces.

Though praise opens divine mysteries and leads to signal

promotions, it also arouses satanic opposition. The king was tempted into making a huge idol on the Plain of Dura and proclaimed a time of dedication. All the citizens in the land were called upon to worship this heathen image. When the band struck up a tune, this was the cue for everyone to fall down and worship. The alternative was death in the fiery furnace. Again, the four Hebrew men refused; their worship was reserved for the God of heaven. (We are not sure why Daniel was not included here. Perhaps he enjoyed official immunity.) Shadrach, Meshach, and Abednego were brought before the king, who was furious with rage over their refusal to bow before his image.

The story is well-known; they were miraculously delivered by a special appearance of One like unto the son of God. The furnace was turned off when the king peered into the flames and saw four men walking among the leaping flames. He welcomed them out of the furnace saying, "Shadrach, Meshach and Abednego, servants of the Most High God, come out! Come here!" (Daniel 3:26). Out they came, their garments not even scorched, their heads not singed, without the smell of smoke. The king responded, "Praise be to the God of Shadrach, Meshach and Abednego, who has sent his angel and rescued his servants!" (Daniel 3:28). The word used here is *barak* which means "to bless." Though praise had brought opposition, it had ultimately caused a heathen king to praise the God of the believers. Hallelujah!

Second, The Effect of Pride When Praise Vanishes

Now we come to the heart of this chapter. We have observed the effects of praise upon a heathen kingdom. Nebuchadnezzar took up the song of praise, and even though he was a heathen, he lifted up his voice in praise to Jehovah. He gave Daniel's three friends great promotions after they had been delivered from the fiery furnace. He even gave a decree that if anyone spoke against the God of the Hebrews, they would surely be cut to pieces and their property reduced to rubble. In subsequent declarations he sounds like a spirit-filled evangelical! "It is my pleasure to tell you about the miraculous signs and wonders that the Most High God has performed for me. How great are his signs, how mighty his wonders! His kingdom is an eternal kingdom; his dominion endures from generation to generation" (Daniel 4:2-3).

After this, King Nebuchadnezzar had another dream, a dream which warned of a dramatic setback. When he told Daniel of the dream, Daniel predicted a coming disappointment which would involve the loss of his kingdom and subsequent restoration. Daniel prophesied, "Seven times [years] will pass by for you until you acknowledge that the Most High is sovereign over the kingdoms of men and gives them to anyone he wishes ... your kingdom will be restored to you when you acknowledge that Heaven rules" (Daniel 4:25*b*-26).

It happened exactly in the way it was foretold. The manner in which it came about is amazing! Nebuchadnezzar's praise for God suddenly ceased and praise for himself began. Twelve months later he was walking on the roof of the royal palace, and he said:

> Is not this the great Babylon I have built as the royal residence, by my mighty power and for the glory of my majesty?" The words were not out of his mouth before the Lord spoke to him, "This is what is decreed for you, King Nebuchadnezzar: Your royal authority has been taken from you. You will be driven away from people and will live with the wild animals; you will eat grass like cattle" (Daniel 4:30-32).

No sooner had God spoken than His word was fulfilled. At that moment, Nebuchadnezzar became insane. This story is an account of the process from sanity to insanity which occurs when one turns from praising God to praising self.

Nebuchadnezzar roamed the forests for seven years until his body was drenched with the dew of heaven, his hair grew like feathers, and his nails became like the claws of a bird. What a price to pay for ceasing to praise!

Third, The Effect of Praise on Insanity

In Nebuchadnezzar's words,

> ...I, Nebuchadnezzar, raised my eyes toward heaven, and my sanity was restored. Then I *praised* the Most High; I *honored* and *glorified* him who lives forever [italics mine]. His dominion is an eternal dominion; his kingdom endures from generation to generation. All the peoples of the earth are regarded as nothing. He does as he pleases with the powers of

> heaven and the peoples of the earth. No one can hold back his hand or say to him: "What have you done?" At the same time that my sanity was restored, my honor and splendor were returned to me for the glory of my kingdom. My advisors and nobles sought me out, and I was restored to my throne and became even greater than before. *Now I, Nebuchadnezzar, praise and exalt and glorify the King of Heaven, because everything he does is right and all his ways are just. And those who walk in pride he is able to humble*" (Daniel 4:34-37, italics mine).

Here is a case where a man merely raised his eyes toward heaven with the intention of praising the God of heaven and he received a healing. Praise is both the cause of sanity being restored and the consequence of sanity restored. The description of this prayer of praise is much like that of Jehoshaphat of old:

1. There was a recognition of God's *exalted position* (He is the Most High whose dominion is eternal).
2. There was a *recounting of His eternal permanence* (His kingdom endures for ever and ever).
3. There was a *review of His predominance* (He does as He pleases).
4. There was a *reference to His excellent power* (no one could hold back His hand).

Thus, we have the unparalleled story of Nebuchadnezzar, the king whose sanity was lost when he stopped praising God and whose sanity was restored when he resumed praise! There is no story like it in literature. It is weighted with significance for us today. All the poison that paralyzes the mind, wrecks the consciousness, and rules the behavior of modern society is bred and grows in an atmosphere which neglects and rebels against God. No praise can originate in insanity. The demons can work unhindered in an atmosphere void of praise. The work of the Holy Spirit is hindered in such an atmosphere.

When we engage in stubbornness, self-pity, jealousy, hate, bitterness, pride, arrogance, and anxiety, sanity may take leave and the seeds of insanity are sown and rooted. We do not have to endure the process through which Nebuchadnezzar passed, but how prone we are to allow pride to stampede roughshod over our lives, unprotested and unchecked—

causing us to become spiritually blind. Repentance and prayer will work humility, though, in the proudest of hearts; and pride will be stopped dead in its arrogant tracks. Sanity is then restored and retained. God remains in His place and we in ours. Order and meaning return to our lives.

Praise dethrones self and enthrones God and His love in the pattern of one's thinking. When God is forgotten, the mind is thrown off-center. When love is restored, God is enthroned in His rightful place. Praise is the ax which cuts at the root of all those disorders which attack us.

Eternity alone will reveal how many people populate the institutions of our land and world who are there because of the absence of praise—and who stay there because it is not introduced. Praise is a therapy almost totally disregarded in the mental welfare of our citizens, yet no therapy would prove as immediately valuable as praise therapy. Whether the "spirit of despair" mentioned in Isaiah 61 is a demon or a human spirit dominated by defeat, the fact remains that praise will neutralize the spirit of despair!

It is time that we, in our continuing study of mental illness, the growing plague of our day, consider seriously the hallelujah factor in both the prevention and treatment of mental illness. It is also time that, in an age of increasing pressures and multiplication of threats to life on earth, we adopt praise as the lifestyle for the preservation of mental balance.

The perspective with which we leave this chapter is the same with which we began the book: God reigns! "The Most High rules in the kingdoms of men. His dominion is eternal and His kingdom endures. He does what He pleases and none can keep Him from it!" (paraphrase of Daniel 4:34-35).

Projects in Praise

1. Mark the references to praise in the Book of Daniel.
2. Memorize Daniel 2:20-21 and use it in personal praise.
3. Read Jeremiah 9:23-24. Note that the KJV translates it, "Let not the wise man glory in his wisdom." The NIV translates the word *glory* as "boast." This is an equivalent of "praise." Make this a personal confession: "I will not boast in anything but the privilege of knowing God!"
4. Read the Book of Daniel with a view to the centrality of praise.
5. Review other praise memory Scriptures.

The Practice of Praise Through Giving

Honor the Lord with your wealth (Proverbs 3:9).

There is an aspect of praise that is a necessary part of the continuing cycle of praise. Without it, the cycle is broken. It is elicited by praise and itself elicits further praise. There may be giving without praise, but there cannot be praise without giving. True praise is always accompanied by giving. The giving spirit is the praising spirit.

One of the high points of any worship service should be the offering. That God would condescend to include man in His enterprises and grant him the privilege of *giving* should be a mind-expanding mystery to the believer. God, who owns the universe and all the wealth in time and eternity, has granted us the grace of giving and thus the privilege of entering into His glorious program—a program as stable as is the sovereignty of God. What a point over which to ponder with praise!

Giving is integral to all praising. When we sing unto the Lord we are giving. When we shout unto the Lord we are giving. When we meditate on the attributes of the Lord we are giving. All worship is, in fact, giving; but ultimately giving will include tangible materials. Money is a medium of exchange which is the distillation of our time, labor, and innovation. When we give, we are not merely giving money, we are giving a part of ourselves, our time, and our talents. We are acknowledging that we belong to God and that this is a normal exercise within the framework of that relationship.

There are two prominent passages I want us to look at in this chapter. The passages are found in 1 Chronicles 29 and 2 Corinthians 8 and 9. These two passages have one uniting theme. They deal with giving as it is connected with praise and thanksgiving. We will move back and forth between these passages as we study this practical aspect of praise.

Building the Temple and Ministering to the Poor

The two cases of giving are not only separated by many centuries but by divergent causes. The amounts of monies mentioned are incomparable, but an interesting fact to note is that in both cases, praise is central.

In 1 Chronicles 29, David is raising the revenue for the glorious Temple which Solomon will build. This is what he tells his people:

> ...Listen to me, my brothers and my people. I had it in my heart to build a house as a place of rest for the ark of the covenant of the Lord, for the footstool of our God, and I made plans to build it. But God said to me, "You are not to build a house for my Name, because you are a warrior and have shed blood" (1 Chronicles 28:2,3).

David set about to challenge Solomon and the people to carry out the instructions God had put in his heart about building the Temple. He then turned to give of his treasures and to challenge the people to give of theirs for the great offering. The magnitude of this offering is best exemplified in the stated amounts of David's personal offering. There were three hundred tons of gold involved, one hundred and ten tons given from David's own personal treasury. Using the present value of gold, David's gift would have been in the neighborhood of one and a half billion dollars! His captains' gifts would have been approximately two and three-fourths billion dollars! That was just the giving which involved gold. There were also four thousand tons of silver given. Today that would be the equivalent of more than sixty-five million dollars! The people also gave in bronze, marble, turquoise, onyx, exotic woods, and other materials to be used in the Temple. What an offering!

The amount of the offering mentioned in 2 Corinthians is minuscule by comparison. It was an offering to the poor and in some cases from the poor. Although the amount was vastly different, the principle was the same. What needed to be done would be done through the giving of those involved. In the first case it involved millions, in the latter pennies. But the background was the same—as was the result—thanksgiving to God!

The Davidic Principle and the Macedonian Example

Praise always presupposes a commitment to the one praised. In the examples above, such commitment is stated as a prerequisite. David challenges, "Now, who is willing to consecrate himself today to the Lord?" (1 Chronicles 29:5*b*). His challenge is both pointed and in the present tense. Paul says of the Macedonians,

> And now, brothers, we want you to know about the grace that God has given the Macedonian churches. Out of the most severe trial, their overflowing joy and their extreme poverty welled up in rich generosity. For I testify that they gave as much as they were able, and even beyond their ability. Entirely on their own, they urgently pleaded with us for the privilege of sharing in this service to the saints. And they did not do as we expected, but *they gave themselves first to the Lord* and then to us in keeping with God's will (2 Corinthians 8:1-5, italics mine).

In both cases the offering of praise was preceded by the giving of self to the Lord.

There are three lofty perspectives given us in these passages from which we may view the high privileges of praise through giving.

First, There is Recognition of God's Sovereign Ownership

The basic principle of our life on earth is that of the sovereign ownership of God. To miss this is to bypass the prime fact of life, its purpose, and destiny. David, in his spontaneous offertory of praise, exulted: "Everything in heaven and earth is yours. Yours, O Lord, is the kingdom; you are exalted as head over all. Wealth and honor come from you; you are ruler of all things" (1 Chronicles 29:11*b*-12). Not only is there a recognition of God's ownership, but of His power to control what He owns.

This same truth comes through several places in the 2 Corinthians passage. In 2 Corinthians 8:9, Paul says, "For you know the grace of our Lord Jesus Christ, that though he was rich, yet for your sakes he became poor, so that you through his poverty might become rich." Everything began with God's ownership and God's riches.

There is another reference which is more subtle but no less significant. Paul springs into an agricultural illustration in 2 Corinthians 9:6 as he says, "Remember this: Whoever sows sparingly will also reap sparingly, and whoever sows generously will also reap generously." In this context Paul makes giving synonymous with sowing. This is of prime importance. What is the means of multiplication? The seed, of course! From whence came the seed? From a previous seed. Repeat that question and its obvious answer ten thousand times or more and you will come back to God's creative act in Genesis 1. Without God there would be no means of sowing and thus no possibility of reaping. The seed is a picture of the sovereignty of God in microcosm! It is also a parable of every believer in whom resides the life of God.

David echoes yet again this vital premise of praise as he shouts in Psalm 24:1, "The earth is the Lord's, and everything in it, the world, and all who live in it." Again he praises in Psalm 89:11, "The heavens are yours, and yours also the earth; you founded the world and all that is in it." God makes this fact clear to Job , when in Job 41:11 He asks, "Who has a claim against me that I must pay? Everything under heaven belongs to me." Again in 1 Chronicles 29:14, David expresses astonishment: "But who am I, and who are my people, that we should be able to give as generously as this? *Everything comes from you, and we have given you only what comes from your hand.*" Later on he says, "O Lord our God, as for all this abundance that we have provided for building you a temple for your holy name, *it comes from your hand, and all of it belongs to you*" (italics mine throughout).

Paul does not let us forget the fact of God's sovereign ownership as he reminds us in 2 Corinthians 9:10, "Now he who supplies seed to the sower and bread for food will also supply and increase your store of seed and will enlarge the harvest of your righteousness."

The reality is this: the great and glorious concept of God's sovereign ownership is the soil in which a harvest of praise begins and in which are planted again and again the seed from praise's rich harvest.

Second, There Is a Reflection on Man's Basic Stewardship

This is the companion truth to that of God's ownership. It is the underlying philosophy in both of our Scripture passages. David is made to understand that he is simply a steward—a temporary custodian—of God's property. Paul reflects on that basic stewardship in the following passage:

> Each man should give what he has decided in his heart to give, not reluctantly or under compulsion, for God loves a cheerful giver. And God is able to make all grace abound to you, so that in all things at all times, having all that you need, you will abound in every good work (2 Corinthians 9:7-8).

Thus the riches of God pass from Him in abundance through us to "every good work." God is the primary owner—we, the distributing stewards. Praise the Lord! Both David and Paul recognize both the responsibility and accountability of basic stewardship. Out of this recognition comes the resolution to exercise the high privilege of giving. David had given out of his personal treasuries. The Macedonians had given out of their deep poverty. Paul reminds us that "each man should give what he has decided in his heart to give" (2 Corinthians 9:7*a*).

Third, There Is a Reception of the Results of Praise through Giving

What happens when we praise through giving? The answer comes from both passages under consideration. It should be remembered that the whole passage in 1 Chronicles 29:10-20 is a spontaneous outcry of praise for the high privilege of giving. It is unparalleled in its loftiness as a doxology of praise. The results were immediate and obvious. A mighty spirit of praise was poured out upon the people. Immediately, "...they all praised the Lord, the God of their fathers; they bowed low and fell prostrate before the Lord and the king" (1 Chronicles 29:20). The chain reaction of results continued as they made sacrifices to the Lord and presented burnt offerings to Him. Later we are told, "They ate and drank with great joy in the presence of the Lord that day" (1 Chronicles 29:22*a*).

Such praise recognizes Biblical order and submission and results in prosperity. The people acknowledged Solomon as their God-appointed leader, and the officers and the mighty men pledged their submission (1 Chronicles 29:23-24). The continuing result was that God prospered Israel and highly exalted Solomon in the sight of all Israel and bestowed on him royal splendor such as no king ever had before (1 Chronicles 29:25).

Paul also expounds on the results of praise through giving. He promises, "You will be made rich in every way so that you can be generous on every occasion, and through us your generosity will result in thanksgiving to God" (2 Corinthians 9:11). He continues by reporting these encouraging words:

> This service that you perform is not only supplying the needs of God's people but is also overflowing in many expressions of thanks to God. Because of the service by which you have proved yourselves, men will praise God for the obedience that accompanies your confession of the Gospel of Christ, and for your generosity in sharing with them and with everyone else. And in their prayers for you their hearts will go out to you, because of the surpassing grace God has given you. Thanks be to God for his indescribable gift! (2 Corinthians 9:12-15).

Look at the accumulated results of praise through giving:

- God's grace abounds toward us in the meeting of every need all the time (2 Corinthians 9:8).
- Every good work is abundantly supported (2 Corinthians 9:8).
- The needs of God's people are supplied (2 Corinthians 9:12).
- This overflows to many expressions of thanks to God (2 Corinthians 9:12*b*).
- The believers' service is approved (2 Corinthians 9:13).
- Because of this, men will praise the Lord! (2 Corinthians 9:13*b*).

Do you see the cycle? It begins in verse 7 with praise through the means of heartfelt giving in a cheerful manner. It is consummated in the giving of praise in verse 13! No wonder Paul responds to this whole matter with a spontaneous doxology, "Thanks be to God for his indescribable gift!" (2 Corinthians 9:15).

Conclusions

The simple conclusion of the whole discussion is this: make your giving an experience of praise! If your church's worship at the time of the offering has become perfunctory and formal instead of worshipful and exciting, take deliberate measures to revise it immediately. I have made some suggestions in a subsequent chapter entitled "Practical Pointers on Public Praise." This time of offering should be one of the mountain peaks of praise during the experience of worship.

If your exercise of giving has become a meaningless ritual, then revise it. Make it a personal, as well as a family, exercise of praise. I have further suggestions on this in the next chapter, entitled "Practical Pointers on Personal Praise."

Projects in Praise

1. Memorize one verse out of each passage discussed in this chapter. Suggestion: 1 Chronicles 29:11; 2 Corinthians 9:8.
2. When you write your check or prepare your gift for giving, stop in the midst of preparations to praise the Lord for the grace of giving. Thank Him for the energy with which to earn that which is about to be given. Thank Him that He has included you in His eternal enterprises.
3. As you give through your church, quietly praise God. It will take on new proportions of joy.
4. Rehearse the results of praise through giving discussed in these two Scripture passages in 1 Chronicles and 2 Corinthians. Hide them in your heart to increase the expectations from giving.
5. Remember that the chief result of praise through giving is the giving of praise! (2 Corinthians 9:13).

16 Practical Pointers on Personal Praise

If you have read this far, surely the last thought in your mind is turning back! You have either browsed the book, read it intently, or have turned to this chapter out of an interest in praise. Ultimately, praise will be no more vital than you allow it to be in the realm of your personal discovery and practice of it.

No doubt you have experienced an urge from within to praise the Lord. That urge lies within every true believer. His Spirit in us is the Spirit of praise. All our redeemed humanity wishes to respond to Him with heartfelt praise. It is our homeland, our natural element. It is where we belong.

We repeat that public praise will never be what it should and can be unless, and until, we learn to enjoy the glories of personal praise.

In our adventure of studying praise at Southcliff, this was the first challenge. The personal theme was adopted from Psalm 119:164: "Seven times a day do I praise thee because of thy righteous judgments" (KJV). I challenged the people to deliberately take *praise breaks* throughout the day. I urged them to become *praise-conscious* and to engage in differing forms of praise under differing circumstances. The determination to praise will be a life-changing experience for anyone who is so committed. If you have read the book to this point and engaged in some or all of the projects in praise, many of these suggestions may have already been implemented. The following concepts are some of the ideas we have learned in our study and practice of personal praise.

What One Determined to Praise May Expect

First, there will be immediate elation. Nothing so touches the sources of the fountains of joy like the exercise of praise. We will soon discover that indeed "the joy of the Lord shall be our strength!" Many have been the reports of immediate joys that have risen when praise is begun. The rise in the joy of public worship is commensurate with that experienced in personal, private worship.

Second, there will be an immediate escalation in spiritual warfare. Almost without exception after the first report of increased joy was the report of an increase in activity on the part of the enemy. The devil hates praise and will do all within his power to thwart it. He has nothing in his arsenal to counteract praise. His purpose is to so attack us that we will abandon our determination to praise. If his attacks on the praiser do not avail, he will attack someone close to the praiser. As I stated in my book *Victory Over the Devil*, "If the devil cannot defeat you, he will try to defeat someone whose defeat will defeat you." It is extremely vital for the praiser to increase his intensity of praise as the battle increases. **The devil cannot long stand against the powerful weapon of praise.** Attacks of depression, physical illness, and opposition from others are not uncommon when praise is exercised. A basic law of revival is this: as God's manifested activity is revealed, the intensity of spiritual warfare will increase accordingly.

Third, there will be an increased perception of spiritual truth. The Bible will come alive. Not only will perception increase, but there is apt to be a prioritization of truths. That is, the most important truths for our particular era in history will rise above others which, while they are vital, are not priority truths for our day. A remarkable reality today is seen in this fact: among those who have made the choice to go on with God, there is a clarifying of vital truths indispensable to reviving the Church. This is happening to people of differing denominations and geographical locations. Praise seems to be a vehicle for Christian unity, a common gathering ground.

Fourth, there will be an increased anticipation and excitement regarding the high privilege of public worship. The significance of gathering the saints, to use the New Testament name for believers, and the joy that accompanies such gatherings will be noticeable. The words of our oldest and grandest hymns will leap off the pages of the hymnbook. New songs, psalms, and spiritual songs will endear themselves to the worshiper. The impact of public Scripture reading and public prayer times will be observable. There will be a change of philosophy concerning the facets of public worship services and their purposes. Hymns which have laid on the pages of the hymnbook unsung for years will come alive with excitement and relevance.

Fifth, there will be a new dimension to the personal quiet time as praise is installed as an integral part of it. Praise will supplant petition, and order will give way to spontaneity. As one becomes acquainted with the elements of praise, the personal worship time will become a *laboratory* in which these newly learned lessons will be applied with joy. There will still be order as well as petition in the quiet time, but worship will make it seem much less like work than before.

Sixth, there will be a fresh and exciting growth in loving God as knowledge of Him increases in the atmosphere of praise. The relationship with Him will be more than a time spent with Him in worship. Life will become a song and service of worship. It will be natural to break forth in joyful laughter and praise as you drive down the highway, wash the dishes, change the baby, or engage in even the most menial of tasks.

S*eventh, praise should become an acquired skill, ever improving, a habit ever stronger in its good grip on us.* While all the above are surely true in all who praise, we are never to allow feelings or sensations, or the absence of them, to alter our habits of praise. We will come to the point where we will choose to praise whether or not we feel like it. It will affect the devil much the same whether we do it out of spontaneity or deliberate and planned intention. It will glorify God as much when we struggle with every opinion and judgment within us to praise as when every sensation within us cries, "Hallelujah!" Like any other exercise, we become more adept with practice. The more we praise, the more natural it becomes to us. Practice moves us toward perfection.

Practical Pointers

1. ***Develop a pure heart.*** I have made it a habit for years of adopting a passage of Scripture for the whole year in addition to my life's passage. My passage for one year was, "Blessed are the pure in heart for they will see God" (Matthew 5:8). During the year I sought more and more to inquire of God

what it meant to have a pure heart. The Greek word is *katharos* which means "clean" or "clear" The heart that can praise the Lord is an unmixed heart, an undivided heart. Paul implored young Timothy to command certain men not to teach false doctrines or be preoccupied with myths and genealogies. He further counseled, "The goal of this command is love, which comes from a pure heart and a good conscience and a sincere faith" (1 Timothy 1:5). The only heart which can love God fully is the pure one. Praise will encourage the keeping of the heart pure.

2. ***Be sure to give time and attention to memorizing the Word of God, particularly in the area of praise.*** I have found that the best motive for memorizing Scripture is to have a specific purpose in mind for which to utilize that Scripture. In no area is the reward for memorization more immediate than in this area of praise. The Holy Spirit can more readily orchestrate heavenly praises through you if your mind is filled with memorized Biblical praises. For this purpose, I have included at the end of this book not only appendices containing hundreds of praise Scriptures, but also one hundred of the great praise Scriptures of the Bible, primarily for the purpose of memorization. Memorization will implement praise, and praise will undergird memorization.

3. ***Never stop studying praise in the Bible.*** For years now I have been studying praise throughout the Bible. About the time I think I have exhausted the subject, I find another rich vein. Aside from finding this intriguing and enjoyable, I have discovered the subject of praise to be intellectually refreshing and invigorating. Let us commit our lives to a study of earth's and heaven's loftiest exercise!

4. ***Share your discoveries on praise with friends and acquaintances.*** To my sheer delight I am discovering that others are learning the pleasures of praise. I never talk with someone about it without learning something fresh about praise.

5. ***Use the hymnbook in personal praise.*** Sing some of the old songs. Collect chorus sheets and music; some fantastic worship and praise choruses are being written. I hear a new one almost every week, sometimes several. (I am seeking to make a collection of them—words, music, and sound if possible. I hope that I can provide these new choruses to

praise ministers and praise-worship workshops across the country.) Memorize the words to the hymns and choruses for use in your personal time of praise. In learning some of the great praise songs, use the personal pronouns to shift emphasis. Example: "'Tis so sweet to trust in Jesus, just to take Him at His word; just to rest upon His promise, just to know 'Thus saith the Lord'" can be changed to this: "'Tis so sweet to trust You, Jesus, just to take You at Your word; just to rest upon Your promise, just to know 'Thus saith my Lord.'"

"His Name Is Wonderful" can be changed to "Your Name Is Wonderful." "He Is Lord" to "You Are Lord." "To God Be the Glory" may be sung "To You (or Thee) Be the Glory"; "Praise the Name of Jesus" seems to be more intimate with "I Praise Your Name, Lord Jesus."

Remember that the song of Moses in Exodus 15 began with, "I will sing to the Lord." Sing loudly, sing softly, sing on key, sing off key, sing choruses, hymns, psalms, or spiritual songs—but sing! By all means, sing! God inhabits (is at home in) the sung praises (*tehillahs)* of His people.

The psalmist requested, "May my tongue sing of your word, for all your commands are righteous" (Psalm 119:172). What a wonderful manner of worship is provided in the singing of the Scriptures. If you are of such a mind, sing the Scriptures not only as an aid to memorization but as a help in worship. Make up your own tunes. You may surprise yourself with latent composing abilities!

6. ***Employ the names of God detailed in Chapter 5 in personal praise.*** Go through the names and observe your needs in the light of the meaning of His names. He is Jehovah-Jireh for your deficiency (Provider). He is Jehovah-Rophe for your infirmity (Healer). He is Jehovah-Nissi for your warfare (Banner of victory). He is Jehovah-M'Kaddesh for your impurity (Sanctifier). He is Jehovah-Shalom for your disturbances (Peace). He is Jehovah-Rohi for your decisions (Guide and Shepherd). He is Jehovah-Tsidkenu for your sin (Righteousness). He is Jehovah-Shammah for your loneliness (The One who is there). Choose one of His names for your time of praise that fits a pressing, present need.

   Example: "Lord, You are my Shepherd, Jehovah-Rohi. I shall not want. I shall not want for nourishment. You make me to lie down in green pastures. I shall not want for rest. You lead me beside still waters. I shall not want for strength.

You restore my soul. I shall not want for justice and guidance. You guide me in paths of righteousness for Your name's sake: I shall not want for companionship. You are with me. I shall not fear. You are with me in the valley of the shadow. I shall not want for comfort. Your rod and staff, they comfort me. Your goodness and love follow me and I will dwell in Your house forever. I praise You, Jehovah-Rohi."

7. ***Using Chapter 16, employ the promptings in your personal praise time.*** Example: "God, just as Moses and the Israelites praised You, I praise You, for You have triumphed gloriously. You are my strength and song and have become my salvation. I will sing unto You" (from Exodus 15).

Projects in Praise

1. Begin a project of marking your Bible, taking note of reasons to praise. You might want to begin in the Psalms, using this chapter as a help.
2. Memorize five scriptural reasons to praise the Lord. Example: Psalm 118:29:
   "Give thanks unto the Lord, for he is good; His love endures forever (two reasons here). Add others of your own choosing. Other reasons to praise given in the Psalms are found in Psalm 48:1; 52:9; 54:6; 56:13; and Psalm 100:5.
3. Rehearse at least three personal reasons to praise the Lord today.
4. Review your praise memory verses.
5. Review three of the covenant names for God, using them in your praise time today.
6. Name three of God's attributes and praise Him for them. (Examples: holiness, sovereignty, love, righteousness, etc.)

17 Practical Pointers on Public Praise

Praise will prove to be an indispensable factor in a Biblical philosophy of worship. Certain catechisms declare that the purpose of men is to glorify God and enjoy Him forever. There can be no worship without praise. At its heart, worship is an expression of our recognition of the greatness of God. Like love, worship is valid only to the degree that it is expressed. A. W. Tozer, in a little booklet entitled *Worship: the Missing Jewel of the Evangelical Church*, observes the following truth:

> Man was made to worship God. God gave to man a harp and said, "Here above all the creatures I have made and created I have given you the largest harp. I put more strings on your instrument and I have given you a wider range than I have given to any other creature. You can worship Me in a manner that no other creature can." And when he sinned man took that instrument and threw it down in the mud and there it has lain for centuries, rusty, broken, unstrung; and man, instead of playing a harp like the angels and seeking to worship God in all of his activities, is ego-centered and turns in on himself and sulks, and swears, and laughs, and sings, but it's all without joy and without worship.

You and I were made for praise. In praise we are fulfilled and satisfied. It is natural for the redeemed to praise the Lord. Once we have begun to implement praise into our personal relationship with God, we will be eager to make public expressions of praise in corporate worship. Meaningful public praise will be a natural consequence of personal praise.

Setting the Stage for Praise

Many mainline denominations have neglected praise for so long that their members are almost totally illiterate on the subject. This illiteracy, coupled with the present emphasis on praise in some circles, produces a caution which may be a hindrance to praise. In fact, well-intentioned people will often stand in opposition to the first signs of praise, believing that they are actually defending the faith. It will prove impossible, as well as unhealthy, to seek to force congregations into praise without the development of an appreciation of it through Biblical teaching.

A proper philosophy of public worship will prove indispensable in the practice of praise, and it will demand a wise and discerning pastor to gently teach, lead, and implement in matters pertaining to praise. He will know how fast the congregation can move, how quickly they can learn, and how gently genuine praise can be implemented. He will be fair to the fearful, kind to the cautious, and careful with the zealots. He will preach on praise, its philosophy, its perspective, and its practice.

Any spectators in the public worship service will be non-Christians. They are not required to sing since they have no song. “Let those refuse to sing who never knew our God” is the correct instruction from the old song. God is our audience and everything is *te Deum* (to God). The preacher, soloists, and choir are not performing. Thus the congregation is forever delivered from the proneness to judge, grade, or criticize.

We often hear people say, “Well, I just didn’t get much out of the worship service today.” Who told them that this was to be the gauge of a great worship service? They should know that they are there to bless the Lord, not just to be blessed by the Lord. We will discover, to our glad surprise, that when we have blessed the Lord, we ourselves will be doubly blessed.

The pastoral staff, elders, or lay leaders must perceive that they are a worship team. If one is *in charge* of the music; another, the announcements; another, the offering; and yet another, the sermon, the results will be a disjointed service of worship. Everything should fit into the glad symphony of praise. The atmosphere which prompts praise begins with the first note of the instrument as people gather for praise. It will be difficult to excite people about the greatness of God if they have been greeted by a doleful dirge as they have entered the worship place. The musicians are not there to play the organ, piano, and other instruments, but to minister to the Lord. The brass, the strings, and the cymbals are so much noise if they do not elicit worship. The whole music team is there, not to perform but to lead the meaningful worship.

General Suggestions

1. The pastor will need to condition the people for praise by talking about it in an elementary manner. He may have to begin with the kindergarten facts of praise. The what, who, how, and why's of praise need to be plainly declared. Nothing should be assumed.

2. The old hymns of praise form a wonderful starting point for meaningful praise. Every hymnbook has a section or a designation for hymns of praise. Frequently, in such an emphasis, a *flagship* hymn will emerge, that is a hymn which especially endears itself to the congregation as a call to praise. In our case it was a song I had never, to my knowledge, heard before: "Come Christians, Join to Sing, Hallelujah Amen!" With every singing of it the challenge increased. As the orchestra joined in and our people sang it from memory, it was even more meaningful.

3. Great worship choruses should be used. I am amazed that virtually every week I hear a new and fresh chorus of praise and worship. As a *flagship hymn* will often emerge, so it is with a *flagship chorus*.. In our case it was "Our God Reigns". As we discovered the perspective of praise to be the sovereignty of God, it seemed natural that we should remind ourselves at every gathering (and generally at the beginning) that indeed our God reigns!

4. Differing needs are met in Sunday morning praise and Sunday evening praise. It seems that in the developing pattern of praise the Sunday morning service is one in which the greatness of God is the prevailing theme and tends to be more formal. The great hymns and choruses which recognize the greatness of God, His sovereignty, His eternality, and His holiness are in order. Though the morning is more formal, intimacy with God is not to be discouraged. Tender moments of "I love You, Lord, and I lift my voice to worship You, oh my soul rejoice" are in place in any service. Yet the triumphant strains of "A Mighty Fortress Is Our God" are never inappropriate either. On Sunday evening a wider range of appeal to the emotions seems to be in order. Choruses encouraging action and excitement help to implement praise. Medleys of choruses are helpful. For instance, a medley of choruses on the name of Jesus is uplifting. Such choruses as "Praise the Name of Jesus," "There's Something About That Name," "Precious Name" (chorus to hymn, "Take the Name of

Jesus With You"), "Jesus, Name Above All Names," "Beautiful Savior," " Wonderful Lord," "His Name Is Jesus," and others are fitting.

5. It will be helpful to print a special booklet of choruses for use in praise worship. Please keep in mind the copyright laws which prohibit the printing of music without permission. Such permission is not difficult to obtain. I have made it a hobby to pick up these booklets in my travels and keep them in a collection. The result is a fantastic and growing collection of choruses that are vital to praise and worship. The fullest collection of praise choruses was found in an Episcopal church!

6. Our church has found that a *chorus of the month* is a good practice. For that entire month the words to the chorus are printed in the Sunday bulletin, and the chorus is sung at the time of greeting the visitors in every service. This guarantees that the church will learn at least twelve new choruses within the year and fixes those songs in the minds of the worshipers.

7. Have a *Top Twenty* list of both favorite praise hymns and praise choruses. Ask the people to nominate their favorite praise hymns and choruses. This will spark interest in praise music. Take the twenty most nominated hymns and choruses and make a list of them for the congregation. I have done this on a limited basis with music leaders across the country and will list the *Top Twenty* from my survey at the end of this chapter.

Most of these suggestions have to do with music in praise. Other practical suggestions have been saved for later. Music has been dealt with first because it is a mood-setter for praise. Remember it is praise music (*tehillah)* that God inhabits (Psalm 22:3 KJV). It is good to keep in mind that there are varying types of songs that accomplish different purposes. Observe the different kinds of hymns of praise:

Hymns which declare the greatness of God. These are great songs of the faith sung in almost all evangelical persuasions. They are in the third person; thus they are *about* God. Their use stirs our minds and hearts with different facets of God's manifold greatness. Examples of such hymns are: "A Mighty Fortress Is Our God," "To God Be The Glory," "O

Worship the King," "Praise Ye the Triune God," "The Lord Is King," "We Magnify Our God," "All Creatures of Our God and King," "Praise, My Soul, the King of Heaven," "Majestic Sweetness Sits Enthroned," "Come, Christians, Join to Sing," "The Name of Jesus Is So Sweet," and "Crown Him with Many Crowns."

Hymns which speak directly to God. They are in the second person. They accomplish something that the former group does not accomplish, namely, highlighting a relationship. It is not that one is more vital than another; they are both necessary and helpful to worship. Most of the above can be tastefully shifted from the third person to the second person with benefit. Example: "Our Mighty Fortress are You, God." Hymns speaking directly to God are: "How Great Thou Art," "Holy God, We Praise Thy Name," "Holy, Holy, Holy," "Come, Thou Almighty King," "O God, Our Help in Ages Past," "Great God of Wonders," "We Praise Thee, O God, Our Redeemer," "Immortal, Invisible," "Joyful, Joyful, We Adore Thee," "Great Is Thy Faithfulness," and "Jesus, What a Friend of Sinners."

Hymns which move between the second and third person. In other words, they mix praises about God and praises directly to God. Examples are: "Blessed Be the Name" (The third verse is shifted to the second person.) "Fairest Lord Jesus" (Verses one and four are in the second person).

Hymns of personal testimony. These stir the memories regarding the beginning of our relationship with God, His provisions all our lives, or some endearing episode in our journey. Examples: "I Stand Amazed," "O How I Love Jesus," "Since Jesus Came into My Heart," "Blessed Assurance," "I Am Thine, O Lord," "All That Thrills My Soul," "Satisfied," "All That Thrills My Soul Is Jesus." Such hymns are vital to praise, plucking the strings of memories that renew our love for the Lord. In the exercise of going through the hymnbook, my heart has been touched in the simple process of reading the words of the hymns.

Here are some examples of differing kinds of praise choruses:

***Enlistment* choruses.** These declare intentions to praise and call for others to praise. Examples: "I Will Praise Him," "Everybody Sing Praise to the Lord," "Sing Hallelujah," "Wherever I Am I'll Praise Him," "Sing, Make A Joyful Sound," "Clap Your Hands, All Ye People."

***Action* choruses.** These call for accompanying actions from the praiser. They are especially helpful in breaking down feelings of intimidation and self-consciousness. Examples are: "With My Hands Lifted Up," "Thy Lovingkindness Is Better Than Life," "His Banner Over Me Is Love" (with accompanying motions).

***Commitment* choruses.** "Fill Me, Jesus," "Unto Thee, O Lord, Do I Lift Up My Soul," "Jesus, Be the Lord of All," "Father, I Adore You."

***Meditative* choruses.** These songs are reminders of the Lord's presence, the meaning of our worship, and our personal intentions to glorify the Lord. Examples are: "We Have Come into This Place to Magnify His Name and Worship Him," "Into Thy Presence," "The Lord Is in His Holy Temple," "Surely the Presence of the Lord Is in This Place," "Set My Spirit Free That I Might Worship Thee."

***Warfare* choruses.** These songs speak of the struggle and the victory that belongs to us in Christ! "In the Name of Jesus," "He Signed My Deed in His Atoning Blood," "I Have the Victory, You Have the Victory, We All Have the Victory Now," " The Weapons of Our Warfare."

***Testimony* choruses.** These amplify a facet of the personal testimony. "I've Been Redeemed," "I've Got Peace Like a River," "O Say, But I'm Glad," "The Joy of the Lord Is My Strength," "I Feel Good," "The Lord Is My Light."

***Intimate* choruses of worship.** Three such songs have especially blessed my heart. I use them often in private worship. They are beautiful in public worship: "O Lord, You're Beautiful" (Keith Green) "I Love You, Lord," and "Praise You, Father, Thank You Jesus, Holy Spirit, Thank You."

The Use of Scripture in Public Praise

I believe that one of the most effective means of praising the Lord in public or private is through use of the Scriptures. The responsive reading has long been a practice in many churches. The praise leader may wish to have the congregation repeat after him at the beginning of the worship service an intention to praise the Lord. Example: "I will bless the Lord at all times: his praise shall continually be in my mouth. My soul shall make her boast in the Lord: the humble shall hear thereof and be glad. O magnify the Lord with me, and let us exalt his name together" (Psalm 34:1-3 KJV). There are dozens of praise Scriptures which can be used in this manner. We will discuss this further under the paragraph on the Offertory.

The Prayer Time as a Period of Praise

The opening prayer is extremely important and can set the pace for praise. If someone other than the pastor leads in this prayer he should be urged to make his prayer primarily one of praise. Even in the Offertory prayer, praise is in order. If there is a special time for prayer in which people are called to the altar or Lord's Supper table (and I strongly recommend such a practice), as the pastor brings the needs represented to the Lord, he may accompany it with praise that God is able to do exceeding abundantly above all that we may ask or think! The closing prayer or song may profitably suggest that those who have worshipped corporately may continue, through the hours ahead, to worship and praise the Lord in private.

The Offertory as a Time of Praise

What a remarkable opportunity for worship is provided as the offering is taken! Yet most of the time we miss it. This time should never be taken for granted. The pastor with glad anticipation might say the following:

> *And now, with thanksgiving that the Lord has included us in His great kingdom enterprises, we come to give our offerings to the Lord. Let everyone participate in these moments of worship through giving! Would you hold your offering up and repeat after me, "Yours, O Lord, is the greatness and the power and the glory and the majesty and the splendor, for everything in heaven and earth is Yours. Yours, O Lord, is the kingdom; You are exalted as head above all. Wealth and honor come from You; You are ruler over all things. In Your*

hands are strength and power to exalt and give strength to all. Now, our God, we give You thanks and praise Your glorious name. But who am I and who are my people that we should be able to give as generously as this. Everything comes from You, and we have given You only what comes from Your hand."

Thoughts for use in an Offertory prayer should center around the mercy of God who has included us in His plan of economy, His provision of wisdom and energy by which our gifts have been earned, and His ability to carry that which we give Him to the ends of the world in reaching people. Many wonderful Scriptures are appropriate in the time of offering: 2 Corinthians 9:6-8; Revelation 5:12-13; 7:12.

Baptism as an Experience of Praise

Baptism is the celebration of new life in Christ. What an appropriate time to invoke the memories of all saints in attendance of the glad day of their salvation and baptism! Songs of testimony may be interspersed between baptisms. In our church we sang the phrase, "I have decided to follow Jesus, no turning back, no turning back" after each baptism. Other appropriate songs are: "I've Been Redeemed," "Since Jesus Came into My Heart," and "This Is the Day."

The Lord's Supper as a Time for Praise

Once we realize the deep meaning and implications of the Lord's Supper, it will inevitably become a time of praise, a celebration of our covenant relationship with God through the blood of Jesus. In essence, it is the counterpart of the covenant meal occasioned when two parties, having entered into a blood covenant, celebrate their new relationship. We are joined to God by the blood of Jesus, the blood of the everlasting covenant. God is committed to us and we to Him. His shed blood has given us spiritual life. It has brought us who were afar off, because of our sins, into intimacy—in fact, into union with Christ. We are encouraged to celebrate, in the Lord's Supper, our high privilege of finding our sustenance in Him. We ingest the elements representing the body and blood of the Lord, symbolizing our identity with Him, and His with us. What a time to praise Him for His grace revealed through Calvary! The song that comes to me at this moment is this:

O Lord, You're beautiful,
Your face is all I see,
And when Your eyes are on this child
Your grace abounds to me.

Because He has died, we have forgiveness and life. Personal thanks to Jesus are in order.

Thank You Lord, for saving my soul,
Thank You Lord, for making me whole,
Thank You, Lord, for giving to me
Thy great salvation, so full and free.

The joy of the Lord's Supper, or the Covenant Meal, may be greatly enhanced as we remember that it looks in three directions:

It is, first of all, a *commemoration.* It looks backward to the death of Christ, His burial, and resurrection. It reminds us of the day we were regenerated and joined the marvelous family of God. In fact, all the memories since we first met Christ are in order for this time.

It is, second, a *celebration.* It looks to the now and observes current blessings. As the covenant meal is received we remember that as covenant children we have covenant privileges with the Father.

It is, third, an *anticipation.* It looks to the future when we will sit down and fellowship with our Lord at His table in heaven.

There are songs, both hymns and choruses, for all these directions. It seems fitting that these outlooks should be emphasized in every gathering of worship. Proper *commemoration* will release us from guilt. Proper *anticipation* will liberate us from fear. Proper *celebration* will free us from frustration. Praise the Lord!

Let every gathering of the body of Christ be a service of praise. Let every committee meeting begin and end with a prayer of praise. Let every facet of the service, the prelude, the singing, the offering, the quiet moments, the sermon, and the invitation be joined in a gift of praise to the Lord. It is never inappropriate to praise! It is always fitting. Let us declare our praises with the psalmist:

> Praise the Lord. Praise God in his sanctuary; praise him in his mighty heavens. Praise him for his acts of power; praise

him for his surpassing greatness. Praise him with the sounding of the trumpet, praise him with the harp and lyre, praise him with tambourine and dancing, praise him with the strings and flute, praise him with the clash of cymbals, praise him with resounding cymbals. Let everything that has breath praise the Lord. Praise the Lord. (Psalm 150).

Projects in Praise

One simple project: be instructed by Psalm 144:9, "I will sing a new song to you, O God..." Create a new song and sing it unto the Lord. Perhaps it will be easier to find a psalm and set the words to music. You'll find it is exhilarating!

Note: Below are listed the top twenty praise-worship hymns which are the result of a survey taken among ministers of music, seminary classes, and Baptist congregations. This survey was made in 1983, during the earlier stages of what may be called the worship revolution (in my thinking more appropriately referred to as the restoration of Biblical worship!) The top twenty worship hymns would not likely be changed from then to now. I have not included the chorus list in this edition because the choruses have changed drastically. With the advent of renewal in the nineties, a more extreme music has emerged in such areas as intimacy, warfare, and commitment. The use of asterisks denotes ties in the survey. Ties are indicated by the same number of asterisks.

TOP TWENTY PRAISE-WORSHIP HYMNS

"To God Be the Glory"
"How Great Thou Art"
"All Hail the Power"
"Victory in Jesus"
"Amazing Grace"
"Holy, Holy, Holy"
"Blessed Assurance"*
"When I Survey the Wondrous Cross"*
"Glorious Is Thy Name"*
"Praise Him! Praise Him!"*
"Great Is Thy Faithfulness"**
"O for a Thousand Tongues to Sing"**
"Fairest Lord Jesus"* * *
"It Is Well with My Soul"***
"A Mighty Fortress" * *
"He Lives" * * *
"Crown Him with Many Crowns"****
"Sweet, Sweet Spirit"*****
"Come Thou Fount"*****
"Praise to the Lord, the Almighty"*****

18 The Pinnacle of Praise

Lift up your heads, O you gates; be lifted up, you ancient doors, that the King of glory may come in. Who is this King of glory? The Lord strong and mighty, the Lord mighty in battle. Lift up your heads, O you gates; lift them up, you ancient doors, that the King of glory may come in. Who is he, this King of glory? The Lord Almighty—he is the King of glory (Psalm 24:7-10).

We come to the highest peak in the mountain range of praise. From here you can almost see forever! Standing on praise's highest peak gives us a perspective offered by no other lofty height.

This passage in Psalm 24 has been one of intrigue to me for years. For some strange reason I felt at home in it, even before I understood a bit of its background. This lofty passage has three perspectives: First, there is the practical or historical perspective. Second, there is the prophetic perspective. Thus, it is anticipatory and deals with the future. Third, there is the personal perspective, dealing with the present. Let us take a brief look at these three vital perspectives.

The Practical Perspective

The scene for this tremendous epic was set in the early reign of King David. The kingdom was united under him, and Saul's mighty men had become David's mighty men. National wounds had begun to heal. This psalm was probably composed at the time David had the ark of the covenant delivered to its rightful place in the capital city of the kingdom. The ark and its contents formed a powerful, visible symbol of the invisible presence of Almighty God. The symbolic testimony of the last years of King Saul's reign was that the presence of God was not all that important. The ark was not at the center of the nation's life. It was in the house of Abinadab, most likely in a storage room covered over by an ancient tarpaulin of sorts. The last years of Saul's reign were characterized by spiritual and physical disarray and confusion. Now both Saul and Jonathan were dead, and David was King.

One of the first executive decisions of King David is recorded in 1 Chronicles 13, where he says, "Let us bring the ark of our God back to us, for we did not inquire of it during the reign of Saul." How tragic are those last words: "We did not inquire of it." What an admission of neglect in pursuing the will of God! The whole gathered assembly of the common people, the mighty men, the priests, and the Levites were in agreement. A new cart was built and the task was begun. However, the ark was made to be carried on the shoulders of holy men, not man-made structures like the new cart. In the process of moving the ark, one of the oxen stumbled and the ark became unsteady. Uzzah reached out to steady the ark and was smitten dead as he touched it. In fear and anger, David detoured the ark to the house of Obed-Edom, where it remained for about three months. David later realized the mistake he had made in allowing the ark to be transported on a cart instead of on the shoulders of the Levites. He said, "We did not inquire of him about how to do it in the prescribed way" (1 Chronicles 15:13*b*).

Finally, the ark was on its way to the city of David. It was homecoming for God! The scene is a moving and touching one in the eyes of our imagination. David had appointed the Levites to prepare an orchestra of lyres, harps, trumpets, and cymbals to praise the Lord, along with the massive choir. They were to flank the ark on each side as it approached its prepared place. As the ark approached the city with the orchestra and choir in full sound, David could no longer contain his excitement and gratitude. He broke into a dance and joined the march of the ark and the procession accompanying it.

In all likelihood the choir on the outside of the city gate accompanying the ark was matched by a choir of equal size within the gates of the city. Their praise is recorded in Psalm 24.

As the ark and its procession approached the gates of the

city, the command was sung, “Lift up your heads, O you gates; be lifted up, you ancient doors, that the King of glory may come in” (Psalm 24:7).

Then from within, the internal choir sang back in response, “Who is this King of glory?”

From without the external choir would reply, “The Lord strong and mighty, the Lord mighty in battle. Lift up your heads, O you gates; lift them up, you ancient doors, that the King of glory may come in” (Psalm 24:8,9).

Once again from within the question was repeated for effect, “Who is he, this King of glory?”

Finally, from without would come the reply, “The Lord Almighty—he is the King of glory (Psalm 24:10).

Then the mighty gates were opened, the doors were lifted, and the ark was brought into the city amid shouts and songs of praise by the combined choirs and orchestras. It is believed that this was the historical background of Psalm 24.

Now the ark was brought to its prepared place. The true King of Israel—Jehovah God—was in His rightful place. The city was safe. Praise Jehovah! Hallelujah!

The Prophetic Perspective

Psalm 24 also looks forward in anticipation to the second coming of our Lord. The King of Glory will enter His Temple. With the swiftness of the wind He will sweep the kingdoms of the earth under His rule, and His righteousness will cover the earth as waters now cover the sea. The kingdoms of this world will become the kingdoms of our Lord and His Christ, and He shall reign forever and ever. This is reality.

He will appear in robes of flashing brightness and imperial majesty. He is the Lord of Hosts, mighty in battle! This was the prophetic light which shone brightly when the lesser lights were being snuffed out by the mad rulers of the first century A.D. Isaiah declared that One was coming upon whose shoulders the government of the world would be placed, and of the increase of that government there would be no end. That One would be called Wonderful Counselor, Mighty God, Everlasting Father, Prince of Peace (Isaiah 9:6-7). It is around this hope, the certainty of His coming, that all our lives are centered. No wonder it is called the blessed hope!

In the mid-seventeenth century, the Turks sealed the massive Eastern Gate to the old city of Jerusalem. It will not again be opened until it is opened to receive the King of kings and Lord of lords. His welcome will be no less glorious than that accorded the ark when it came into the city. Perhaps again we will hear the words of that same psalm and the orchestras and choirs blending their sounds and voices together in welcoming back the King! Hallelujah!

The Personal Perspective

In the meantime, we can do more than commemorate and anticipate. **We can celebrate because this psalm has a personal and present implication.** Until He comes in visible glory, He is with us in invisible glory. He is prepared to distill the glory of His presence anywhere He is accorded a proper atmosphere. That atmosphere is none other than praise. At this precise point is the pinnacle of praise, when our praises have been thus pleasing to Him and He comes in manifest presence. This can happen in your personal praises and mine, as well as in the services of corporate worship—and that will be the peak, the highest point in the whole range of praise. Into that rarefied atmosphere of praise, He will come in glory to consume the worshiper in joy, baptize the Body in love, and anoint the Body of Christ with power.

I want to break the psalm down into four parts so that you and I can put it into practice right where we are.

1. *The Invitation to Proceed.* "Lift up your heads, O you gates; be lifted up, you ancient doors." We are the gates and the doors that open and lift for the coming of the King. Actions are demanded, detailed, and repeated. Our praises are the opening of the doors and the lifting of the gates. That is our primary role. What a sobering thought to know that we can encourage His coming and manifest His presence or we can be the closed doors and gates who keep Him out. It all centers around our praises!

2. *There Is the Promised Incoming.* The underlying truth throughout all this episode is that God actually wants to enter and reveal Himself to His people. "And the King of glory shall come in" (KJV)! That promise is good today, whether in the quiet of our personal prayer room or in the corporate worship service with

other saints of God. He is waiting, poised in all His glorious power to enter into our circumstances. His incoming will produce change on every hand. The King will be in residence and will demonstrate His sovereign rule.

3. *The Identity Pursued.* "Who is this King of glory?" The answer is a dual one. First, **He is identified by His exalted position.** He is the Lord, strong and mighty. He reigns. We are back to our praise orientation—God on a throne and a mighty service of worship. Second, **He is identified by His efficient performance.** He is the Lord, mighty in battle.

4. *Implications Perceived.* We sing a song, "The Lord is in His holy temple, The Lord is in His holy temple; Let all the earth keep silence before Him, Keep silence, keep silence before Him." The King is present, prominent, and powerful. He has taken over the nation. He is glad to take us under His reign.

We have dealt with the last four verses of Psalm 24. Now we return to the verses preceding them. The vital questions are asked, "Who may ascend the hill of the Lord? Who may stand in his holy place?" And the answer comes back clearly, "He who has clean hands and a pure heart, who does not lift up his soul to an idol or swear by what is false." That is a simple qualification for those who desire to stand at the pinnacle of praise, the hill of the Lord, His holy place. And that which gives us the right to ascend gives us the right to stay on the mountain peak of praise.

Finally, there is the promise to those who thus stand, "He will receive blessing from the Lord and vindication from God his Savior" (Psalm 24:5). So it will be with all those who seek the Lord.

As the reader gives personal application to this chapter, let it be known that just as a city or a church has gates and doors, so do we. Our emotions, our voices, our arms, our hands, and our eyes are the gates and doors through which the Lord comes in blessed presence into our situations.

Yes, He is already there even as He was in the kingdom of David. But when He is welcomed, when the doors are lifted and the gates are opened, He comes in a manner in which He has not come before, to do what He has never before done: that is revival!

Projects in Praise

1. Memorize Psalm 24:7-10. This is vital. I do not know a greater passage for memory in the Word of God!
2. As you memorize it, use it in your prayer time over and over again.
3. Keep notes on what impressions the Lord gives you of its implications.
4. If you can, turn it into a song.
5. As you come into personal worship, ask yourself the vital questions of Psalm 24:3, reading the answers in the next verse. Make it a habit to ask these questions:
   A. Are my hands clean?
   B. Is my heart pure?
   C. Have I lifted up my soul to an idol?
   D. Have I sworn by anything false?
6. Picture yourself standing on the pinnacle of praise in the hill of the Lord, His holy place. Stand there in quietness for a while enjoying the view!

19 Postscripts on Praise

I have been somewhat haunted while writing this book by the repeated thought that more could have been added to every chapter. This would be the case even after a hundred revisions in writing on praise. I am keenly aware that we have only touched the hem of the garment in our study.

At this point I am deeply grateful for a journalistic invention referred to as a postscript or *P.S.* I do not know what the inventor of this innovation had in mind when it was initiated, nor do I know his name. My impression is, however, that a postcript is identified as a word one wishes to say after the main body of writing has been written. If that is so, then this chapter is aptly named, for it contains many ideas that might have been added to the main body of writings. Even after the writing of this chapter, there will be other thoughts which come to mind. I will simply have to save the rest for other volumes to follow. Please know that the placement of these postscripts does not suggest lesser value but such value that they merit final consideration.

A Classic Testimony

In many cases where praise is rediscovered there will be traumatic transitions in relationships and directions. I present the case of John Wyatt, the minister of music and productions who was, suddenly and without warning, converted into John Wyatt, minister of praise. Here is his story in the first person:

> Big bucks and big productions with lots of theatrics and showmanship characterized the ministry of music for me. I wasn't deeply satisfied with that direction, but it was all I knew. I wanted God to use me to make an impact, and the big productions provided the way as far as I knew or could imagine. Bigger and better dreams were on the drawing board for the future, and everything was go for even bigger bucks

and bigger productions.

Then came traumatic Friday, the day of the budget planning committee in 1978. The priorities of our church were changing and I was all for it. I just didn't know what all it was going to mean. What it meant was that my music budget was cut in half from over $50,000! I was stunned; I saw the necessity of it and the impossibility of it at the same time. I felt like I had been slammed to the floor by a giant who had grabbed me by the feet. My mental faculties were short-circuited. I was immobilized. I could hear the devil shouting, "Resign!" I imagined that I could hear choir members screaming and crying over dashed expectations. I did not see how the music ministry could possibly survive the sudden change in direction. I said to the budget planning committee, "The meeting is over as far as I am concerned!" I just couldn't handle it. The chairman of the meeting understood and adjourned the meeting.

I went home, got out my papers and my calculator, and formed a puddle of pity with my tears. How could this be? My ministry had ended! The day before I had been full of optimism and motivated by bigger and better dreams. Suddenly it was all over! As I sat there grinding over the figures, another voice began whispering in my ear. It said, "Let's take a walk in the mountains." After another hour or so feeling sorry for myself, I yielded to the voice.

At that time I lived in the mesa at the foot of the Sandia Mountains of Albuquerque, New Mexico. I drove to one of those trails and began the climb. The freshness of the mountain air began clearing away the cobwebs of doubt and despair.

I began to remember my trust in God and His past faithfulness. I remembered that I could count on Him to guide my ministry through the authority structures in my life. As the trail began to twist back and forth up the mountain toward the north crest, my faith was revived. I said, "Father, I believe You brought me here to this place. You put me on this staff. You gave me this pastor." It wasn't easy but I said, "I freshly submit my life to You. I know that You are guiding me through what is happening to me right now. Father, I believe that You are up to something and quite honestly, Lord, I would appreciate it ever so much if You would tell me what You are doing." Somehow I knew that someday I would know. I could still see nothing, but I knew that I was standing on the Rock!

To my surprise, God began to speak to my heart clearly. I remember the exact spot. I recently showed it to a dear friend. God said, "John, today I'm changing your name. You are no longer John Wyatt, minister of music and productions. You are now John Wyatt, minister of worship and praise!" My heart bolted. I knew that I was on holy ground. The darkness was suddenly light. I began to shout and cry. The pressure of the climb was gone. I couldn't even feel the steepness of the mountain trail.

As I moved up the trail I began to see the new things God had for me. He indicated that the program would dip at first until the people caught on. But they would catch on. He said, "If I can get you to give your whole life to worship and praise, don't you think I can get people to give a few hours of their time to help you? Your choirs will get bigger and better but will cost less and less. They will operate at a different pace but will serve a better purpose." As I continued my hike I enjoyed the beautiful sense of God's presence. He began to tell me what I was to say to the people. He literally spelled out the first steps in the new game plan. I could see it as if it had already happened and I was excited beyond measure.

I left the mountain and headed for the phone. The first thing I wanted to do was to call my pastor and tell him what God had told me. I wanted him to know how grateful I was for his courage and how grateful I was to God for directing my ministry through his leadership.

And now, years later, all that God showed me that day has happened. The blessings that come from praising God exceed the limit of the best words that might be used to describe them. The psalmist said, "Blessed are they that learn to acclaim You, O Lord." According to that Scripture one can learn to praise the Lord. In reality, praising God was something that I had to begin learning to do. I began to see that praising God is a must for me and a must for every believer who really wants to go on with God. Praise is precious to God and powerful to the praiser. Almost daily God has guided me to new truths about praise. That would have been blessing enough! But the highest joy of all is ministering among God's people and seeing them learn to praise and adore their Lord and to walk in the unparalleled blessing of it all. "Praise You, Lord, I love You and adore You."

I feel that many stories like this will be told with varying degrees of trauma in transition and with comparative results of joy and success! Amen, John!

An Atheist's Testimony on Blasphemy

Blasphemy is the opposite of praise, for those who blaspheme hurl epithets Godward. Dedicated atheists actually discipline themselves to blaspheme God. A woman who had delved deeply into the mysteries of praise was moved to attend a meeting where a certain converted atheist was giving testimony of his conversion. He related that he and his atheist friends would gather in their meetings and take turns publicly blaspheming God. They were so adeptly trained that they could stand for hours and hurl the most hideous of insults and ridicule toward God without ever repeating themselves. They were blatant, arrogant, and totally free from self-consciousness. They seemed to have a demonic anointing in their diabolical doings that was literally out of this world—and very likely it was!

The woman later testified that she was smitten with the thought of a tragedy. These atheists admittedly did not believe in God and yet, ironically, were so committed and disciplined to blaspheme Him—while millions of saints seemed almost totally unconcerned about praising Him at all!

What a blessing it would be if we believers could be so committed to the discipline of praise that we could stand for hours lost in praise, glorifying God in lofty phrases without so much as repeating ourselves. So it is and so shall it be in heaven! "It is not the dead who praise the Lord, those who go down to silence; it is we who extol the Lord both now and forevermore. Praise the Lord (Psalm 115:17-18). "Praise be to the Lord forever!" (Psalm 89:52). Such a glorious prospect for eternity should motivate us to initiate and intensify the adventure now!

Phrases Worth Repeating

Praise is an impenetrable defense before the enemy and an indefensible weapon in spiritual warfare. God is restoring praise to His church and with it the graces that will make the Bride-elect both bride-conscious and bride-beautiful!

Praise is at once the most powerful tonic for a tired soul and the greatest therapy for a heavy spirit. Praise is the church's secret weapon against which the enemy has no defense and before which his ranks fall into confusion and disarray. Praise douses doubts and waters faith at the same time.

Praise is a powerful disinfectant that kills on contact a myriad of germs which are allowed to proliferate in a praiseless atmosphere. Praise crowns obedience and puts the praiser over into the victory column. Praise will preface the return of Christ, pervade the rapture, and surround the events of the end time as life on earth gives way to timeless eternity when the rivers of history flow into the boundless Sea of Forever.

While praise is the highest of spiritual exercises, it is something we **become** before it is something we **do**. Our lives first become songs of praise. Then out of our lives issue meaningful songs of praise. Praise is a decisive down-payment and plays the greatest role in mental health and emotional stability. Praise, like a straight line, is the shortest distance between a saint and his God!

The Final Word

This book and the Bible will have at least one thing in common; they will end in the same word. Of all the omissions, I have been most haunted by that of *AMEN*! For some strange reason I have successfully resisted the temptation to insert it here or there. Not until now did I understand why. Now I know it was because it belonged here at the end of the work.

The word *amen* is found more than twenty-five times in the Old Testament and more than 125 times in the New. It means and sounds much the same in both Hebrew and Greek as in English. It means "sure, steadfast, and permanent." It is translated many times in the New Testament "verily, verily" and beckons unlimited belief.

Most significantly, for our observation, *amen* is a word of praise. It is a word of agreement. In 1 Chronicles 16:36 the people responded to great praises with "Amen" and "Praise the Lord." It is a word of finality.

"Praise be to the Lord, the God of Israel from everlasting to everlasting. Amen and Amen" (Psalm 41:13).

The grace of the Lord Jesus be with God's people. Hallelujah! Amen!

Appendix A

Presuppositions in Praise

The principles we have discussed proceed from certain presuppositions. It is only fair that the reader should have these at their disposal. I list them as follows:

God is Restoring Praise to the Body of Christ All Over the World

It is happening! It is a work of God! No one can stop it! It has been a long time in coming. The drought has been lengthy and wearisome, but the sounds of the abundance of rain are beginning to be heard.

Praise the Lord for groups springing up everywhere who seem to have led out in praise. It has been easier for them since they had no precedents to limit them. We may not agree on all points of doctrine, but all who know the Lord are happy to agree on the glorious fact that *our Lord is worthy to be praised.*

Praise Is the Most Worthwhile Endeavor in Earth and Heaven

An exercise which ceaselessly occupies the angels in heaven and in which heavenly citizens will engage in eternity surely could not be a waste of time to mortals on earth. One may be sure that time spent in praise will never prove to be time wasted but will, in fact, prove all else done in the light of it more worthwhile. There are at least four basic ministries for the body of Christ in general and the believer in particular. They are the ministry of WORSHIP, the ministry of the WORD, the ministry of WITNESS, and the ministry of WORK. It is my conviction that the key to a proper balance in these vital ministries is placing WORSHIP in its rightful priority position.

No Exercise Will Result in More Healing Physically, Mentally, Emotionally, and Spiritually Than That of Studying and Practicing Praise

In our laboratory of praise within the local church we discovered that long-standing hang-ups disappeared as folks began to praise the Lord on a continuing basis. The reasons for this have become obvious as you have already read.

The Practice of Praise in the Corporate Sense Is Absolutely Indispensable to the Maximum Worship Experience

We may preach and plead with people to repent, be cleansed, be committed, and follow the Lord, but few will make lasting commitments without a prevailing atmosphere of praise. We may plead with men and women to receive Christ and crown Him as Lord, but their maturity is an unlikely goal unless we surround them in the early stages of their Christian experience with praises to God.

Until the Practice of Praise in Private Is Continuous and Free, the Practice of Praise Corporately Will Be Inhibited by Fear, Self-consciousness, and Discomfort

Public praise is threatening and fearful to those who are not "into" praise in their private lives. I would encourage the reader to continue what I hope you have begun in the projects in praise—practice of praise in its simplicity. Out of that will flow a desire, expectations, and delight toward public exercises in praise.

When We Praise, We Are Engaging in an Eternal Exercise

Paul declares in Romans 1:25 that God is "forever praised." We shall discover that praise is eternal. It never began. It has always been. It will never cease. The psalmist recognized this fact as indicated in Psalm 72:19, "Praise be to his glorious name forever." He further declared, "Then will I ever sing praises to your name" (Psalm 61:8). Still further he claims in Psalm 111:10*b*, "To him belongs eternal praise."

Our Practice of Praise Will Improve As We Learn the Biblical Truth About It

I have never appreciated more than now the implications of John 8:32: "Then you will know the truth, and the truth will set you free." True believers cannot be chided, cajoled, and jerked into the practice of the truth. One does not have to engage in a manipulative, high-pressure, determined campaign to convince people of the worth of praise. The preaching of the truth will do the job! When the truth is heard, heeded, and applied there will be freedom in that area. Someone has thoughtfully theorized, "We tend to be down on what we are not up on!" I have watched folks move from fear to faith under the preaching of simple Biblical truths.

Observe the Scriptures below. Repeat them several times. Memorize which appeal to you most. Set these as your "morning exercises."

> I will extol the Lord at all times; his praise will always be on my lips. My soul will boast in the Lord; let the afflicted hear and rejoice. Glorify the Lord with me; let us exalt his name together (Psalm 34:1-3).
>
> Then will I ever sing praise to your name and fulfill my vows day after day (Psalm 61:8).
>
> My mouth is filled with your praise, declaring your splendor all day long (Psalm 71:8).
>
> Seven times a day I praise you for your righteous laws (Psalm 119:164).
>
> Praise the Lord. How good it is to sing praises to our God, how pleasant and fitting to praise him! (Psalm 147:1)
>
> Let everything that has breath praise the Lord. Praise the Lord! (Psalm 150:6)
>
> Seven times a day I praise you for your righteous laws (Psalm 119:164).

Appendix B

Prominent Praise Passages in the Scriptures

Author's Note: I am including these at the end of the book because of the immense pleasure these praise passages have been in my own practice of praise. I trust that they will be helpful to the reader. This is by no means an exhaustive list of such passages but simply a number of key scriptures on the subject of praise. (An even hundred!)

> I will sing to the Lord, for he is highly exalted. The horse and its rider he has hurled into the sea. The Lord is my strength and my song; he has become my salvation. He is my God, and I will praise him, my father's God, and I will exalt him (Exodus 15:1*b*,2).

> I will proclaim the name of the Lord. Oh, praise the greatness of our God! He is the Rock, his works are perfect, and all his ways are just. A faithful God who does no wrong, upright and just is he (Deuteronomy 32:3,4).

> When the princes in Israel take the lead, when the people willingly offer themselves—praise the Lord! Hear this, you kings! Listen, you rulers! I will sing to the Lord, I will sing; I will make music to the Lord, the God of Israel (Judges 5:2,3).

> ...My heart rejoices in the Lord; in the Lord my horn is lifted high. My mouth boasts over my enemies, for I delight in your deliverance. There is no one holy like the Lord; there is no one besides you; there is no Rock like our God (Samuel 2:1,2).

> ...The Lord is my rock, my fortress and my deliverer; my God is my rock, in whom I take refuge, my shield and the horn of my salvation. He is my stronghold, my refuge and my savior... (2 Samuel 22:2,3)

> The Lord lives! Praise be to my Rock! Exalted be God, the Rock, my Savior! (2 Samuel 22:47)

> Therefore I will praise you, O Lord, among the nations; I will sing praises to your name (2 Samuel 22:50).

...O Lord, God of Israel, enthroned between the cherubim, you alone are God over all the kingdoms of the earth. You have made heaven and earth (2 Kings 19:15).

Give thanks to the Lord, call on his name; make known among the nations what he has done. Sing to him, sing praise to him; tell of all his wonderful acts. Glory in his holy name; let the hearts of those who seek the Lord rejoice (1 Chronicles 16:8-10).

Sing to the Lord, all the earth; proclaim his salvation day after day. Declare his glory among the nations, his marvelous deeds among all peoples. For great is the Lord and most worthy of praise; he is to be feared above all gods (1 Chronicles 16:23-25).

Ascribe to the Lord, O families of nations, ascribe to the Lord glory and strength, ascribe to the Lord the glory due his name. Bring an offering and come before him; worship the Lord in the splendor of his holiness (1 Chronicles 16:28,29).

Let the heavens rejoice, let the earth be glad; let them say among the nations, "The Lord reigns!" Let the sea resound, and all that is in it; let the fields be jubilant, and everything in them! Then the trees of the forest will sing, they will sing for joy before the Lord, for he comes to judge the earth (1 Chronicles 16:31-33).

Praise be to the Lord, the God of Israel, from everlasting to everlasting. Then all the people said "Amen" and "Praise the Lord" (1 Chronicles 16:36).

...Praise be to you, O Lord, God of our father Israel, from everlasting to everlasting. Yours, O Lord, is the greatness and the power and the glory and the majesty and the splendor, for everything in heaven and earth is yours. Yours, O Lord, is the kingdom; you are exalted as head over all (1 Chronicles 29:10,11).

Wealth and honor come from you; you are the ruler of all things. In your hands are strength and power to exalt and give strength to all. Now, our God, we give you thanks, and praise your glorious name (1 Chronicles 29:12,13).

After consulting the people, Jehoshaphat appointed men to sing to the Lord and to praise him for the splendor of his holiness as they went out at the head of the army, saying: "Give thanks to the Lord, for his love endures forever." As they began to sing and praise, the Lord set ambushes against the men of Ammon and Moab and Mount Seir who were invading Judah, and they were defeated (2 Chronicles 20:21,22).

...Stand up and praise the Lord your God, who is from everlasting to everlasting. Blessed be your glorious name, and may it be exalted above all blessing and praise (Nehemiah 9:5).

God is exalted in his power. Who is a teacher like him? Remember to extol his work, which men have praised in song. How great is God—beyond our understanding! The number of his years is past finding out (Job 36:22,24,26).

But you are a shield around me, O Lord, my Glorious One, who lifts up my head (Psalm 3:3).

I will give thanks to the Lord because of his righteousness and will sing praise to the name of the Lord Most High (Psalm 7:17).

O Lord, our Lord, how majestic is your name in all the earth! You have set your glory above the heavens. From the lips of children and infants you have ordained praise because of your enemies, to silence the foe and the avenger (Psalm 8:1,2).

I will praise you, O Lord, with all my heart; I will tell of all your wonders. I will be glad and rejoice in you; I will sing praise to your name, O Most High (Psalm 9:1,2).

The Lord reigns forever; he has established his throne for judgment. Sing praises to the Lord, enthroned in Zion; proclaim among the nations what he has done (Psalm 9:7,11).

But I trust in your unfailing love; my heart rejoices in your salvation. I will sing to the Lord, for he has been good to me (Psalm 13:5,6).

I will praise the Lord, who counsels me; even at night my heart instructs me. I have set the Lord always before me. Because he is at my right hand, I will not be shaken. Therefore my heart is glad and my tongue rejoices; my body also will rest secure (Psalm 16:7-9).

You have made known to me the path of life; you will fill me with joy in your presence, with eternal pleasures at your right hand (Psalm 16:11).

I love you, O Lord, my strength. The Lord is my rock, my fortress and my deliverer; my God is my rock, in whom I take refuge. He is my shield and the horn of my salvation, my stronghold (Psalm 18:1,2).

The Lord lives! Praise be to my Rock! Exalted be God my Savior! He is the God who avenges me, who subdues nations under me, who saves me from my enemies. You exalted me above my foes; from violent men you rescued me. Therefore I will praise you among the nations, O Lord; I will sing praises to your name (Psalm 18:46-49).

Be exalted, O Lord, in your strength; we will sing and praise your might (Psalm 21:13).

Yet you are enthroned as the Holy One; you are the praise of Israel (Psalm 22:3).

I will declare your name to my brothers; in the congregation I will praise you. You who fear the Lord, praise him! All You descendants of Jacob, honor him! Revere him, all you descendants of Israel! (Psalm 22:22,23)

The Lord is my light and my salvation—whom shall I fear? The Lord is the stronghold of my life—of whom shall I be afraid? (Psalm 27:1)

Praise be to the Lord, for he has heard my cry for mercy. The Lord is my strength and my shield; my heart trusts in him, and I am helped. My heart leaps for joy and I will give thanks to him in song. The Lord is the strength of his people, a fortress of salvation for his anointed one (Psalm 28:6-8).

Ascribe to the Lord, O mighty ones, ascribe to the Lord glory and strength. Ascribe to the Lord the glory due his name; worship the Lord in the splendor of his holiness (Psalm 29:1,2).

Rejoice in the Lord and be glad, you righteous; sing, all you who are upright in heart! (Psalm 32:11)

Sing joyfully to the Lord, you righteous; it is fitting for the upright to praise him. Praise the Lord with the harp; make music to him on the ten-stringed lyre. Sing to him a new song; play skillfully, and shout for joy (Psalm 33:1-3).

I will extol the Lord at all times; his praise will always be on my lips. My soul will boast in the Lord; let the afflicted hear and rejoice. Glorify the Lord with me; let us exalt his name together (Psalm 34:1-3).

I will give you thanks in the great assembly; among throngs of people I will praise you (Psalm 35:18).

My tongue will speak of your righteousness and of your praises all day long (Psalm 35:28).

Delight yourself in the Lord and he will give you the desires of your heart (Psalm 37:4).

He put a new song in my mouth, a hymn of praise to our God. Many will see and fear and put their trust in the Lord (Psalm 40:3).

Praise be to the Lord, the God of Israel, from everlasting to everlasting. Amen and Amen (Psalm 41:13).

In God we make our boast all day long, and we will praise your name forever (Psalm 44:8).

I will perpetuate your memory through all generations; therefore the nations will praise you for ever and ever (Psalm 45:17).

Clap your hands, all you nations; shout to God with cries of joy. How awesome is the Lord Most High, the great King over all the earth! (Psalm 47:1,2)

Great is the Lord, and most worthy of praise, in the city of our God, his holy mountain (Psalm 48:1).

I will praise you forever for what you have done; in your name I will hope for your name is good. I will praise you in the presence of your saints (Psalm 52:9).

But I will sing of your strength, in the morning I will sing of your love; for you are my fortress, my refuge in times of trouble. O my Strength, I sing praise to you; you, O God, are my fortress, my loving God (Psalm 59:16,17).

Because your love is better than life, my lips will glorify you. I will praise you as long as I live, and in your name I will lift up my hands (Psalm 63:3,4).

Shout with joy to God, all the earth! Sing to the glory of his name; offer him glory and praise! (Psalm 66:1,2)

May the peoples praise you, O God; may all the peoples praise you. May the nations be glad and sing for joy, for you rule the peoples justly and guide the nations of the earth (Psalm 67:3-5).

I will praise God's name in song and glorify him with thanksgiving (Psalm 69:30).

Praise be to the Lord God, the God of Israel, who alone does marvelous deeds. Praise be to his glorious name forever; may the whole earth be filled with his glory. Amen and Amen! (Psalm 72:18,19)

I will praise you, O Lord my God, with all my heart; I will glorify your name forever. For great is your love toward me; you have delivered my soul from the depths of the grave (Psalm 86:12,13).

I will sing of the Lord's great love forever; with my mouth I will make your faithfulness known through all generations (Psalm 89:1).

Come, let us sing for joy to the Lord; let us shout aloud to the Rock of our salvation. Let us come before him with thanksgiving and extol him with music and song (Psalm 95:1,2).

Sing to the Lord a new song; sing to the Lord, all the earth. Sing to the Lord, praise his name; proclaim his salvation day after day. Declare his glory among the nations, his marvelous deeds among all peoples (Psalm 96:1-3).

Enter his gates with thanksgiving and his courts with praise; give thanks to him and praise his name. For the Lord is good and his love endures forever; his faithfulness continues through all generations (Psalm 100:4,5).

Praise the Lord, O my soul; all my inmost being, praise his holy name. Praise the Lord, O my soul, and forget not all his benefits (Psalm 103:1,2).

Praise the Lord, you his angels, you mighty ones who do his bidding, who obey his word. Praise the Lord, all his heavenly hosts, you his servants who do his will. Praise the Lord, all his works everywhere in his dominion. Praise the Lord, O my soul (Psalm 103:20-22).

Give thanks to the Lord, call on his name; make known among the nations what he has done. Sing to him, sing praise to him; tell of all his wonderful acts. Glory in his holy name; let the hearts of those who seek the Lord rejoice (Psalm 105:1-3).

Praise the Lord. Praise, O servants of the Lord, praise the name of the Lord. Let the name of the Lord be praised, both now and forevermore. From the rising of the sun to the place where it sets the name of the Lord is to be praised (Psalm 113:1-3).

Praise the Lord, all you nations; extol him, all you peoples. For great is his love toward us, and the faithfulness of the Lord endures forever. Praise the Lord (Psalm 117:1,2).

Accept, O Lord, the willing praise of my mouth, and teach me your laws (Psalm 119:108).

Seven times a day I praise you for your righteous laws (Psalm 119:164).

May my lips overflow with praise, for you teach me your decrees. May my tongue sing of your word, for all your commands are righteous (Psalm 119:171,172).

Praise the Lord, all you servants of the Lord who minister by night in the house of the Lord. Lift up your hands in the sanctuary and praise the Lord (Psalm 134:1,2).

I will praise you, O Lord, with all my heart; before the "gods" I will sing your praise. I will bow down toward your holy temple and will praise your name for your love and your faithfulness, for you have exalted above all things your name and your word (Psalm 138:1,2).

I will exalt you, my God the King; I will praise your name for ever and ever. Every day I will praise you and extol your name for ever and ever. Great is the Lord and most worthy of praise; his greatness no one can fathom (Psalm 145:1-3).

Praise the Lord. Praise the Lord, O my soul. I will praise the Lord all my life; I will sing praise to my God as long as I live (Psalm 146:1,2).

Praise the Lord. How good it is to sing praises to our God, how pleasant and fitting to praise him! (Psalm 147:1)

Praise the Lord. Praise God in his sanctuary; praise him in his mighty heavens. Praise him for his acts of power; praise him for his surpassing greatness (Psalm 150:1,2).

Let everything that has breath praise the Lord. Praise the Lord (Psalm 150:6).

In that day you will say: "Give thanks to the Lord, call on his name; make known among the nations what he has done, and proclaim that his name is exalted. Sing to the Lord, for he has done glorious things; let this be known to all the world. Shout aloud and sing for joy, people of Zion, for great is the Holy One of Israel among you" (Isaiah 12:4-6).

O Lord, you are my God; I will exalt you and praise your name, for in perfect faithfulness you have done marvelous things, things planned long ago (Isaiah 25:1).

Sing to the Lord a new song, his praise from the ends of the earth, you who go down to the sea, and all that is in it, you islands, and all who live in them. Let the desert and its towns raise their voices; let the settlements where Kedar lives rejoice. Let the people of Sela sing for joy; let them shout from the mountain tops. Let them give glory to the Lord and proclaim his praise in the islands (Isaiah 42:10-12).

For as the soil makes the sprout come up and a garden causes seeds to grow, so the Sovereign Lord will make righteousness and praise spring up before all nations (Isaiah 61:11).

... Praise be to the name of God for ever and ever; wisdom and power are his. He changes times and seasons; he sets up kings and deposes them. He gives wisdom to the wise and knowledge to the discerning. I thank and praise you, O God of my fathers... (Daniel 2:20, 21, 23)

Then I praised the Most High; I honored and glorified him who lives forever. His dominion is an eternal dominion; his kingdom endures from generation to generation (Daniel 4:34*b).*

But I, with a song of thanksgiving, will sacrifice to you. What I have vowed I will make good. Salvation comes from the Lord (Jonah 2:9).

Yet I will rejoice in the Lord, I will be joyful in God my Savior. The Sovereign Lord is my strength; he makes my feet like the feet of a deer, he enables me to go on the heights (Habakkuk 3:18,19*a).*

"At that time I will deal with all who oppressed you; I will rescue the lame and gather those who have been scattered. I will give them praise and honor in every land where they were put to shame. At that time I will gather you; at that time I will bring you home. I will give you honor and praise among all the peoples of the earth when I restore your fortunes before your very eyes," says the Lord (Zephaniah 3:19,20).

And Mary said: "My soul praises the Lord and my spirit rejoices in God my Savior" (Luke 1:46,47).

Praise be to the Lord, the God of Israel, because he has come and has redeemed his people (Luke 1:68).

Oh, the depth of the riches of the wisdom and knowledge of God! How unsearchable his judgments, and his paths beyond tracing out! "Who has known the mind of the Lord? Or who has been his counselor? Who has ever given to God, that God should repay him?" For from him and through him and to him are all things. To him be the glory forever! Amen (Romans 11:33-36).

Now to him who is able to establish you by my gospel and the proclamation of Jesus Christ, according to the revelation of the mystery hidden for long ages past...to the only wise God be glory forever through Jesus Christ! Amen (Romans 16:25,27).

Praise be to the God and Father of our Lord Jesus Christ, who has blessed us in the heavenly realms with every spiritual blessing in Christ (Ephesians 1:3).

Now to him who is able to do immeasurably more than all we ask or imagine, according to his power that is at work within us, to him be glory in the church and in Christ Jesus throughout all generations, for ever and ever! Amen (Ephesians 3:20,21).

Rejoice in the Lord always. I will say it again: Rejoice! Let your gentleness be evident to all. The Lord is near (Philippians 4:4,5).

Now to the King eternal, immortal, invisible, the only God, be honor and glory for ever and ever. Amen (1 Timothy 1:17).

Through Jesus, therefore, let us continually offer to God a sacrifice of praise—the fruit of lips that confess his name (Hebrews 13:15).

But you are a chosen people, a royal priesthood, a holy nation, a people belonging to God, that you may declare the praises of him who called you out of darkness into his wonderful light (1 Peter 2:9).

To him who is able to keep you from falling and to present you before his glorious presence without fault and with great joy—to the only God our Savior be glory, majesty, power and authority, through Jesus Christ our Lord, before all ages, now and forevermore! Amen (Jude 24,25).

You are worthy, our Lord and God, to receive glory and honor and power, for you created all things, and by your will they were created and have their being (Revelation 4:11).

...Worthy is the Lamb, who was slain, to receive power and wealth and wisdom and strength and honor and glory and praise! (Revelation 5:12)

...Amen! Praise and glory and wisdom and thanks and honor and power and strength be to our God for ever and ever. Amen! (Revelation 7:12)

...Great and marvelous are your deeds, Lord God Almighty. Just and true are your ways, King of the ages. Who will not fear you, O Lord, and bring glory to your name? For you alone are holy. All nations will come and worship before you, for your righteous acts have been revealed (Revelation 15:3,4).

After this I heard what sounded like the roar of a great multitude in heaven shouting: "Hallelujah !Salvation and glory and power belong to our God" (Revelation 19:1).

The twenty-four elders and the four living creatures fell down and worshipped God, who was seated on the throne. And they cried: "Amen, Hallelujah!" Then a voice came from the throne, saying: "Praise our God, all you his servants, you who fear him, both small and great!" (Revelation 19:4,5)

Then I heard what sounded like a great multitude, like the roar of rushing waters and like loud peals of thunder, shouting: "Hallelujah! For our Lord God Almighty reigns. Let us rejoice and be glad and give him the glory! For the wedding of the Lamb has come, and his bride has made herself ready" (Revelation 19:6,7).

Appendix C

Promptings to Praise

I realized early on that my study should include a search for reasons to praise the Lord. I thought if I were able to discover fifty different reasons to praise the Lord I would be fortunate. I discovered to my delight that there were over 230 different reasons to praise the Lord in the Scriptures. I am simply going to list those reasons with the Scripture references.

1. Moses and the Israelites praised the Lord because He had gloriously triumphed. (Exodus 15:1)
2. God had thrown their enemies with their horses into the sea. (Exodus 15:1)
3. He was their strength and their song and had become their salvation. (Exodus 15:2)
4. God was their God and their fathers' God; thus they praised and exalted Him. (Exodus 15:2)
5. They sang unto the Lord because He was highly exalted. (Exodus 15:21)
6. Jethro praised the Lord because He, the Lord, rescued the Israelites from the hand of the Egyptians. (Exodus 18:10)
7. Moses praised the Lord in song because of His greatness, because He was a rock, His ways were perfect, and all His ways were just. (Deuteronomy 32:3,4)
8. He further praised God because He did no wrong, being upright and just. (Deuteronomy 32:4*b*)
9. Deborah and Barak praised the Lord because the people offered themselves willingly to the Lord. (Judges 5:2)
10. The women praised God for Naomi's kinsman-redeemer in Boaz. (Ruth 4:14)
11. Hannah praised the Lord because He had lifted her horn (strength) high. (1 Samuel 2:1)
12. David praised the Lord with a dance because the ark, the visible symbol of the presence of God, was being brought to its rightful place. (2 Samuel 6:14,15)
13. David praised the Lord because He was worthy of praise and saved him from his enemies. (2 Samuel 22:4)

14. He praised the Lord further because He avenged him and put nations under him, exalting him above his foes and rescuing him from violent men. (2 Samuel 22:48,49)
15. David praised the Lord because He had shown him the successor to his throne in Solomon, his son. (1 Kings 1:48)
16. Solomon praised the Lord because He had fulfilled what He had promised to his father, David. (1 Kings 8:15)
17. He further praised the Lord because He had given rest to His people, Israel. (1 Kings 8:56)
18. The queen of Sheba praised because God had delighted in Solomon and had placed him on the throne of Israel. (1 Kings 10:9,10)
19. Asaph and his associates praised the Lord because of His wonderful acts and His holy name. (1 Chronicles 16:9,10)
20. They added praises because God was great and worthy of praise. (1 Chronicles 16:25)
21. Heman and Jeduthun and the rest of those designated to praise the Lord sang His praises because His love was enduring. (1 Chronicles 16:41)

No less than ten reasons are found to praise the Lord in David's offertory praise in 1 Chronicles 29:

22. God's greatness
23. God's power
24. God's glory
25. God's majesty
26. God's splendor
27. God's ownership
28. God's exalted headship
29. God's being the source of wealth and honor
30. God, the ruler of all things
31. His hands have strength and power to exalt and give strength.
32. Hiram, king of Tyre, praised the Lord because He had made heaven and earth. (2 Chronicles 2:12)
33. The most frequently mentioned reason for praising the Lord is His enduring love. (2 Chronicles 7:3,6; 20:21)
34. Jehoshaphat appointed men to sing praises to God for the splendor of His holiness. (2 Chronicles 20:21)
35. The people of Ezra's day praised the Lord because the foundation of the house of the Lord was laid. (Ezra 3:11)
36. The people of Nehemiah's day praised the Lord because He had given them great joy. (Nehemiah 12:43)
37. Job praised the Lord because He had given and taken away. (Job 1:21)

The Psalms contain many reasons to praise the Lord:

38. Because of His righteousness (Psalm 7:17)
39. Because of the enemies, to silence the foe and the avenger (Psalm 8:2)
40. Because God is enthroned in Zion (Psalm 9:11)
41. Because He has been good (Psalm 13:6)
42. Because He counsels His own (Psalm 16:7)
43. Because He is at the right hand and stability results (Psalm 16:8)
44. He is worthy of praise (Psalm 18:3)
45. He avenges and subdues nations (Psalm 18:47)
46. He gives great victories (Psalm 18:50)
47. He shows great kindness to David and his descendants forever (Psalm 18:50)
48. He has heard the cry for mercy (Psalm 28:6)
49. He is the strength and shield (Psalm 28:7)
50. He is trustworthy and helps His own (Psalm 28:7)
51. The Lord is the strength for His people and a fortress of salvation for His anointed (Psalm 28:8)
52. He lifted them out of the depths (Psalm 30:1)
53. He did not let their enemies gloat over them (Psalm 30:1)
54. His anger lasts only for a moment, His favor for a lifetime (Psalm 30:5)
55. He has shown His wonderful love (Psalm 31:21)
56. It is fitting for the upright to praise Him (Psalm 33:1)
57. His word is right and true (Psalm 33:4)
58. He is faithful in all He does (Psalm 33:4*b*)
59. He is the King of all the earth (Psalm 47:7)
60. Because He is great and greatly to be praised (Psalm 48:1)
61. For this God is our God for ever and ever (Psalm 48:14).
62. Because He will be our guide even to the end (Psalm 48:14*b*)
63. Because of what He has done (Psalm 52:9)
64. Because His name is good (Psalm 54:6)
65. Because He has delivered the soul from death, the feet from stumbling (Psalm 56:13)
66. Because His love is great, reaching unto the heavens (Psalm 57:10)
67. Because His faithfulness reaches unto the skies (Psalm 57:10*b*)
68. Because He is a fortress and a refuge in times of trouble (Psalm 59:16)
69. Because His love is better than life (Psalm 63:3)
70. Because He is our help (Psalm 63:7)
71. Because He has preserved us and kept our feet from slipping (Psalm 66:9)
72. Because He has not rejected our prayer (Psalm 66:20)
73. Because He has not withheld His love (Psalm 66:20)
74. Because He rules the people justly (Psalm 67:4)

75. Because He guides the nations with justice (Psalm 67:4)
76. Because He daily bears our burdens (Psalm 68:19)
77. Because praise pleases the Lord more than an ox or a bull with its horns and hoofs (Psalm 69:31)
78. Because God will save Zion and rebuild the cities of Judah–then people will settle there and possess it; the children of His servants will inherit it, and those who love His name will dwell there (Psalm 69:35,36)
79. Because of His faithfulness (Psalm 71:22)
80. Because those who wanted to do harm have been put to confusion (Psalm 71:24)
81. Because He alone does marvelous deeds (Psalm 72:18)
82. Because His name is near (Psalm 75:1)
83. Because His love is great and He has delivered the soul from the depths of the grave (Psalm 86:13)
84. Because He is our glory and strength and by His favor He exalts our horn (strength) (Psalm 89:17)
85. Because it is good to praise the Lord (Psalm 92:1)
86. Because of the greatness of His works (Psalm 92:4,5*a*)
87. Because of the profundity of His thoughts (Psalm 92:5*b*)
88. Because the Lord is a great God and King above all gods (Psalm 95:3)
89. Because in His hand are the depths of the earth, and the mountain peaks belong to Him (Psalm 95:4)
90. Because the sea is His, for He made it, and His hands formed the dry land (Psalm 95:5)
91. Because He is our God and we are the people of His pasture, the flock under His care (Psalm 95:6,7)
92. Because of His greatness and worth, He is to be feared above all gods (Psalm 96:4)
93. Because He comes to judge the earth in righteousness and His people in His truth (Psalm 96:13)
94. Because He has done marvelous things (Psalm 98:1)
95. Because His right hand and His holy arm have worked salvation for him (Psalm 98:1*b*)
96. Because He has made known His salvation and has revealed His righteousness to the nations (Psalm 98:2)
97. Because He has remembered His love and His faithfulness to the house of Israel (Psalm 98:3)
98. Because the Lord our God is holy (Psalm 99:9)
99. Because of His goodness, love, and faithfulness (Psalm 100:5)
100. Because of His love and justice (Psalm 101:1)
101. Because He forgives all our sins (Psalm 103:3)
102. Because He heals all our diseases (Psalm 103:3*b*)

103. Because He redeems our lives from the pit and crowns us with compassion and love (Psalm 103:4)
104. Because He satisfies our desires with good things so our strength is renewed like the eagle's (Psalm 103:5)
105. Because He is clothed with splendor and majesty, wraps Himself in light as with a garment, and stretches out the heavens like a tent (Psalm 104:1,2)
106. Because He makes the clouds His chariots and rides the wings of the wind (Psalm 104:3)
107. Because He makes the winds His messengers and His ministers flames of fire (Psalm 104:4)
108. Because He sets the earth on its foundations and it can never be moved (Psalm 104:5)
109. Because of His unfailing love, His wonderful deeds in satisfying the thirsty and filling the hungry with good things (Psalm 107:8,9). The above prompting to praise is repeated in Psalm 107:5,21, and 31.
110. Because He stands at the right hand of the needy one to save his life from those who condemn him (Psalm 109:31)
111. Because great are His works, pondered by all who delight in them (Psalm 111:2)
112. Because He has caused His wonders to be remembered (Psalm 111:4)
113. Because He is gracious and compassionate (Psalm 111:4*b*)
114. Because He provides food for those who fear Him (Psalm 111:5)
115. Because He remembers His covenant forever (Psalm 111:5*b*)
116. Because He has shown His people the power of His works, giving them the lands of other nations (Psalm 111:6)
117. Because the works of His hands are just and faithful (Psalm 111:7)
118. Because He has provided redemption for His people and ordained His covenant forever (Psalm 111:9)
119. Because to Him belongs eternal praise (Psalm 111:10)
120. Because He is exalted over all the nations, His glory above the heavens (Psalm 113:4)
121. Because He raises the poor from the dust and lifts the needy from the ash heap, and seats them with the princes of the people (Psalm 113:7,8)
122. Because He settles the barren woman in her home as a happy mother of children (Psalm 113:9)

The most frequently given persuasions to praise the Lord are His great love and enduring faithfulness. These are repeated in Psalm 115:1; Psalm 117:2; and Psalm 118:1, 29.

123. Because He answered prayer and brought salvation (Psalm 118:21)
124. Because this is the day the Lord has made (Psalm 118:24)
125. Because of His righteous laws (Psalm 119:62,164)

126. Because He teaches His decrees (Psalm 119:171)
127. Because all His commands are righteous (Psalm 119:172)
128. Because He has not let us be torn by the teeth of our enemies (Psalm 124:6)
129. Because the Lord has done great things for us (Psalm 126:2,3)
130. Because praise is good and pleasant (Psalm 135:3)
131. Because the Lord has chosen Jacob to be His own and Israel to be His treasured possession (Psalm 135:4)

In Psalm 136 God's goodness and love are again the theme. In each of these twenty-six verses one of God's attributes or works is extolled with the refrain "His love endures forever" occurring after every statement. Remember that in 2 Chronicles 20 Jehoshaphat and his army had this cry on their lips as they went into battle: "Give thanks to the Lord, for his love endures forever" (v. 21). Evidently, of all the reasons to praise the Lord, this one is paramount! It may well be the one most easily forgotten.

132. Because the glory of the Lord is great (Psalm 138:5)
133. Because we are fearfully and wonderfully made (Psalm 139:14)
134. Because He trains our hands for war and our fingers for battle (Psalm 144:1)
135. Because He gives victory to kings and delivers His servant David from the deadly sword (Psalm 144:10)

In Psalm 145 there is a summary of persuasions to praise that have already been mentioned in other places. He is great and most worthy of praise (v. 3). He is a God of glorious splendor and majesty (v. 5). His works are wonderful (v. 5*b*). He is a God of great power and awesome works (v. 6). His goodness is abundant and He is righteous (v. 7). He is gracious and compassionate, slow to anger and rich in love (v. 8). His kingdom is glorious (v. 11). His kingdom and dominion are everlasting (v. 13). He is faithful to all His promises and loving toward all He has made (v. 13*b*). He upholds the fallen and those with bowed heads (v. 14). He opens His hand and satisfies every living thing (v. 16). He is righteous in all His ways and is near to all who call upon Him (vv. 17,18). He fulfills the desires of those who fear Him, hears their cries, and saves them (v. 19). He watches over all who love Him, destroying the wicked (v. 20).

136. Because the Lord reigns forever (Psalm 146:10)

137. Because it is good, pleasant, and fitting to praise the Lord (Psalm 147:1)
138. Because the Lord delights in those who fear [praise] Him (Psalm 147:11)
139. Because He strengthens the bars of the gates of Zion and blesses the people within it (Psalm 147:13)
140. Because He grants peace to its borders and satisfies with the finest wheat (Psalm 147:14)
141. Because He commanded and everything was created (Psalm 148:5)
142. Because He set everything in place and gave a decree that it will never pass away (Psalm 148:6)
143. Because He takes delight in His people and crowns the humble with salvation (Psalm 149:4)
144. Because praise (along with the Word) inflicts vengeance on the nations, punishments on the people, binds their kings with fetters, their nobles with shackles of iron, carries out the sentence written against them (Psalm 149:6-9)
145. Because of His acts of power (Psalm 150:2*a*)
146. Because of His surpassing greatness (Psalm 150:2*b*)
147. The seraphim praise the Lord because He is holy and His glory fills the earth (Isaiah 6:3)
148. Because great is the Holy One of Israel among you (Isaiah 12:6)
149. Because in perfect faithfulness He has done marvelous things (Isaiah 25:1)
150. Because the fear [praise] of the Lord is the key to His treasures (Isaiah 33:6)
151. Praise is the reason that we have been formed (Isaiah 43:21)
152. Because the Lord has redeemed Jacob and displays His glory in Israel (Isaiah 44:23)
153. Because praise delays God's wrath (Isaiah 48:9)
154. Because the Lord comforts His people and has compassion on His afflicted ones (Isaiah 49:13)
155. Because the Lord has comforted His people and has redeemed Jerusalem (Isaiah 52:9)
156. Because the Lord will bare His holy arm in the sight of all the nations and all the ends of the earth will see the salvation of our God (Isaiah 52:10)
157. Because the Lord has provided praise as a garment to be put on for the spirit of despair (Isaiah 61:3)
158. Because He has clothed us with garments of salvation and arrayed us with robes of righteousness (Isaiah 61:10)
159. Because His righteousness and praise will spring up before all nations (Isaiah 61:11)
160. We are to praise because in praise we see His joy (Isaiah 66:5)

161. We are to praise [boast] because we know Him, the Lord (Jeremiah 9:24)
162. Because giving glory to God will prevent the darkness of judgment in which the feet will stumble (Jeremiah 13:16)
163. Because He rescues the needy from the hand of the wicked (Jeremiah 20:13) Again in Jeremiah 33:11 is the recurring reason to praise the Lord, "...for the Lord is good; and his love endures forever"

Daniel praised the Lord:

164. Because wisdom and power are His (Daniel 2:20)
165. Because He changes the times and the seasons and sets up kings and deposes them (Daniel 2:21)
166. Because He gives wisdom to the wise and knowledge to the discerning (Daniel 2:21*b*)
167. Because He reveals the deep and hidden things; He knows what lies in darkness (Daniel 2:22)
168. Because light dwells with Him (Daniel 2:22)
169. Because He had given to Daniel wisdom and power and made known to him what he asked for (Daniel 2:23)

Nebuchadnezzar praised the Lord:

170. Because He had delivered Shadrach, Meshach, and Abednego out of the fiery furnace (Daniel 3:28)
171. Because of the miraculous signs and wonders He had performed (Daniel 4:2)
172. Because His kingdom is an eternal kingdom and His dominion endures from generation to generation (Daniel 4:3)
173. Because all the peoples of the earth are regarded as nothing (Daniel 4:35)
174. Because He does as He pleases with the powers of heaven and the people of the earth, and none can hold back His hand or say, "What have You done?" (Daniel 4:35)
175. Because everything God does is right and all His ways are just, and those who walk in pride He is able to humble (Daniel 4:37)

The prophets praised Him:

176. Joel suggested praise because God had given the people a teacher for righteousness (Joel 2:23)
177. Habakkuk rejoiced in the Lord because He made his feet like the feet of a deer, enabling him to go on the heights (Habakkuk 3:19)
178. Zephaniah implored Israel to praise the Lord because their punishment had been taken away and their enemies had been turned back (Zephaniah 3:15)

179. Zechariah records God saying, “Shout and be glad, O Daughter of Zion. For I am coming, and I will live among you” (Zechariah 2:10). Later in Zechariah 9:9 the Messiah’s coming calls for rejoicing and shouting, “Rejoice greatly, O Daughter of Zion! Shout, Daughter of Jerusalem! See, your king comes to you, righteous and having salvation, gentle and riding on a donkey, on a colt, the foal of a donkey”

His coming brings several other reasons to praise:

180. He will bring peace to the nations (Zechariah 9:10)
181. He will extend his rule worldwide (Zechariah 9:10*b*)
182. He will set the prisoners free and restore twice as much to them (Zechariah 9:11,12)

Mary, highly favored of God, praised the Lord:

183. Because He had been mindful of His servant and that from now on all generations would call her blessed (Luke 1:48)
184. Because the Mighty One had done great things for her ... holy is His name (Luke 1:49)
185. Because His mercy extended to those who fear Him, from generation to generation (Luke 1:50)
186. Because He had performed mighty deeds with His arm; He scattered those who were proud in their inmost thoughts (Luke 1:51)
187. Because He had brought down rulers from their thrones but lifted up the humble (Luke 1:52)
188. Because He had filled the hungry with good things but had sent the rich away empty (Luke 1:53)
189. Because He had helped His servant Israel, remembering to be merciful to Abraham and his descendants forever (Luke 1:54,55)

Others praised God:

190. Zechariah praised the Lord because God had come to redeem His people, raising up a horn of salvation (Luke 1:68,69)
191. The shepherds praised God for what they had heard and seen (Luke 2:20)
192. Simeon praised the Lord because he had seen salvation prepared by the Lord in sight of all people (Luke 2:30,31)
193. Anna the prophetess praised the Lord because of the child who would bring redemption (Luke 2:38)
194. The paralytic praised God because he was healed (Luke 5:25)
195. The people praised God when they saw the paralytic healed and praising God (Luke 5:26)
196. Jesus praised the Lord because He had hidden things from the wise and learned and had revealed them to children (Matthew 11:25, Luke 10:21)

197. Jesus instructed us to rejoice in opposition from men because our reward is great in heaven (Luke 6:23)
198. The crippled woman praised God because she was healed and was able to straighten up (Luke 13:13)
199. The leper praised God in a loud voice because his leprosy was gone (Luke 17:15)
200. The blind man praised God because his sight was given (Luke 18:43)
201. The people praised God because they saw the whole episode (Luke 18:43)
202. In the triumphal entry the people began to praise God in loud voices for all the miracles they had seen (Luke 19:37)

The Pharisees rebuked their praising and asked Jesus to stop them. Jesus gave us another reason to praise the Lord.

203. Because if we do not praise the Lord the rocks will do it for us (Luke 19:40)
204. The centurion at the foot of the cross praised God because he perceived that Jesus was a righteous man (Luke 23:47)
205. The cripple at the gate called "Beautiful" began to walk, leap, and praise God because he was healed (Acts 3:8,9)

Paul praised the Lord:

206. In his service to God (Romans 15:17)
207. Because God is the Father of compassion and God of all comforts who comforts us so that we may comfort others (2 Corinthians 1:3,4)
208. Because of His indescribable gift [the grace of giving] (2 Corinthians 9:15)
209. Paul praised (boasted) in his weakness that the power of Christ might rest on him (2 Corinthians 12:9)
210. He praised again (delighted) in weaknesses and the like because when he was weak, he was strong (2 Corinthians 12:10)
211. Because God has blessed us with all spiritual blessings in heavenly places in Christ Jesus (Ephesians 1:3)
212. Because Jesus had given him strength, considered him faithful, and appointed him to His service (1 Timothy 1:12)
213. Because he anticipated that the Lord would rescue him from every evil attack and would bring him safely to His heavenly kingdom (2 Timothy 4:18)

And still others praise Him:

214. The writer of Hebrews exhorts us to praise God continually because Jesus had suffered for us to make us holy (Hebrews 13:13-15)

215. We praise because this is the reason that we have become a royal priesthood, a holy nation, a people belonging to God, having been delivered out of darkness into His marvelous light (1 Peter 2:9)
216. We are to rejoice and praise that we can participate in the sufferings of Christ so we may be overjoyed in the later glory revealed, praising God that we bear His name (1 Peter 4:13-16)

The Book of Revelation gives us reasons to praise the Lord:

217. Because God is holy, almighty, and eternal (Revelation 4:8)
218. Because He is worthy to receive glory, honor, and power (Revelation 4:11)
219. Because He created all things and for His "pleasure they are and were created" (Revelation 4:11 KJV)
220. Because the Lamb (Christ) is worthy to receive power, wealth, wisdom, strength, glory, honor, and praise (Revelation 5:12)
221. Because salvation belongs to our God who sits on the throne and to the Lamb (Revelation 7:10)
222. Because the Lord God Almighty has taken His great power and has begun to reign (Revelation 11:17)
223. Because the hour of judgment had come (Revelation 14:7)
224. Because He alone is holy, all nations will come and worship Him, and His righteous acts have been revealed (Revelation 15:4)

In Revelation 19 there are several praises framed in four great hallelujahs:

225. Because salvation, glory, and power belong to our God (Revelation 19:1*b*)
226. Because His judgments are true and just (Revelation 19:2)
227. Because His servants have been avenged and the great prostitute has been judged (Revelation 19:2)
228. Because the Lord God Almighty reigns (Revelation 19:6)
229. Because the wedding of the Lamb has come and the Bride has made herself ready, wearing the fine linen of righteous acts (Revelation 19:7,8)
230. John exhorted praise (worship) because the testimony of Jesus is the spirit of prophecy (Revelation 19:10)
231. The last-recorded praise in the Bible adds one more reason to praise the Lord—Jesus is coming soon. "Amen. Come, Lord Jesus." (Revelation 22:20)

Appendix D
Thirty Days to Greater Praise

I want to suggest a day-by-day plan to a life of greater praise. I have heard that it takes about twenty-one days to solidify a good habit. For good measure, let's make it thirty days! Your praise project is to begin this thirty-day praise exercise. Simply use these pages of the book as your guide during the next thirty days. Surely, at the end of that period your adventure in personal praise will have only begun!

DAY ONE: Read 2 Samuel 22:47-50

Rehearse God's name, Jehovah-Jireh: Our Provider. Speak to Him as your Provider. Memorize Philippians 4:19. Personalize it. "You, my God, are meeting all my needs according to your riches in glory by Christ Jesus." Refer to the second stanza of the poem at the end of Chapter 5.

DAY TWO: Read 1 Chronicles 16:23-28

Rehearse God's name, Jehovah-Rophe: Our Healer. Address Him as your healer. Mention any ailment as you praise Him as healer. Mention any emotional wound or deep regret from the past. Memorize Psalm 107:20. ("He sent forth his word and healed them; he rescued them from the grave.") "Lord, I thank You that You are sending Your word and healing me; You are rescuing me from the grave." Review your memory verses. Refer to the third stanza of the poem at the end of Chapter 5.. Personalize the verse: "Praise Jehovah-Rophe, praise Jehovah-Rophe, You're my Health, You're my Healing, You're my Physician; in You do I trust. Praise Jehovah-Rophe."

DAY THREE: Read 1 Chronicles 29:10-13

Rehearse God's name, Jehovah-Nissi. Look to Him as your Banner of Victory. Praise Him that He has made you a super conqueror. Memorize Romans 8:37. Personalize it: "Lord, I thank

You that in all these things I am more than a conqueror through You who loved me." Refer to the fourth stanza of the poem at the end of Chapter 5. Review the previous memory verses.

DAY FOUR: Read Psalm 3:3, 4; 5:1-3

Rehearse God's name, Jehovah-M'Kaddesh. Look to Him as your Sanctifier. Praise Him that He has made you a true and genuine saint! Memorize Leviticus 20:8. Personalize it: "Lord, I will keep Your decrees and follow them, for You are Jehovah who makes me holy!" Refer to the fifth stanza of the poem at the end of Chapter 5. Review previous memory verses.

DAY FIVE: Read Psalm 9:1, 2, 7, 11

Rehearse God's name, Jehovah-Shalom. Look to Him as your Peace. Memorize Psalm 119:165. Personalize it: "I have great peace because I love Your law and nothing causes me to stumble." Refer to the sixth stanza of the poem at the end of Chapter 5. Review your memory work.

DAY SIX: Read Psalm 16:7-11

Rehearse God's name, Jehovah-Rohi. Look to Him as your Shepherd. Memorize Psalm 16:11. Say aloud, "God, you have made known to me the path of life; you will fill me with joy in your presence, with eternal pleasures at your right hand." Refer to the seventh stanza of the poem at the end of Chapter 5. Review your memory work.

DAY SEVEN: Read Psalm 18:1-3

Rehearse God's name, Jehovah-Tsidkenu. Look to Him as your Righteousness. Memorize 2 Corinthians 5:21. Personalize it: "Lord, I thank You that Jesus was made sin for me, that I might be made the very righteousness of God in Christ Jesus." Refer to the eighth stanza of the poem at the end of Chapter 5. Review previous memory work.

DAY EIGHT: Read Psalm 24:7-10

Rehearse the last name of God: Jehovah-Shammah. Look to Him as the Ever-present One, always there. Memorize Revelation 4:8*b*. "Holy, holy, holy is the Lord God Almighty, who was, and is, and is to come." Refer to the ninth stanza of the poem at the end of Chapter 5. Review past memory work.

DAY NINE: Read Psalm 28:6-8; 29:1-5

Read or sing the great praise song: "My Jesus, I Love Thee".

My Jesus, I love Thee, I know Thou art mine,
For Thee all the follies of sin I resign.
My gracious Redeemer, My Saviour art Thou,
If ever I loved Thee, My Jesus, 'tis now.

I love Thee because Thou has first loved me
And purchased my pardon on Calvary's tree.
I love Thee for wearing the thorns on Thy brow.
If ever I loved Thee, My Jesus, 'tis now.

I love Thee in life, I love Thee in death,
I love Thee as long as Thou givest me breath.
And say when the death dew lies cold on my brow
If ever I loved Thee, My Jesus, 'tis now.

In mansions of glory and endless delight
I'll ever adore Thee in mansions so bright.
I'll sing with the glittering crown on my brow
If ever I loved Thee, My Jesus, 'tis now.

Memorize 1 John 4:16. Personalize it: "Lord, I know and rely on the love You have for me. You are love and I, living in love, live in You and You in me." Review previous memory work.

DAY TEN: Read Psalm 33:1-4

Read or sing "Jesus, What a Friend of Sinners." The tune is *Hyfrydol*, Welsh in origin. (See hymnal.)

Jesus, what a friend of sinners,
Jesus, lover of my soul,
Friends may fail me, foes assail me,
You, my Saviour make me whole.

Hallelujah, what a Saviour,
Hallelujah, what a Friend,
Saving, helping, keeping, loving,
You are with me to the end.

Memorize Psalm 40:3. Personalize it: "Lord, You have put a new song in my mouth, a hymn of praise to our God. Many will see and fear and put their trust in the Lord." Review past memory work.

DAY ELEVEN: Read Psalm 34:1-4

Praise the Lord, using Psalm 29 as it appears in Spurgeon's *Our Own Hymnbook.*

Ascribe to God, ye sons of men,
Ascribe with one accord,
All praise and honour, might, and strength,
To Him, the Living Lord!
Give glory to His holy Name,
And honour Him alone;
Give worship to His majesty,
And bow before His throne.
The Lord doth sit upon the floods,
Their fury to restrain;
He reigns above, both Lord and King,
And evermore shall reign.
The Lord shall give His people strength,
And bid their sorrows cease;
The Lord shall bless His chosen race,
With everlasting peace.

Memorize Psalm 41:13. Personalize it: "I praise You, Lord God of Israel, from everlasting to everlasting. Amen and Amen!" Review past memory work.

DAY TWELVE: Read Psalm 46:10

Memorize today's psalm. Spend five minutes in silence, meditating on the last half of that verse: "I will be exalted among the nations, I will be exalted in the earth." Silence can be praise! Review all past memory verses.

DAY THIRTEEN: Read Psalm 63:3-5

Today, our word is *hallal*, the root of hallelujah. It means to laud, boast, or rave. Laud or boast about God to His face. Brag on Him for a few minutes with every compliment you can recall. Example: "Lord, You are very great. Your name is a strong tower. I can run to it and be safe. You have been our dwelling place from generation to generation. From everlasting to everlasting You are God. You are great and greatly to be praised. Yours is the strength, honor, glory, majesty, and blessing forever and ever. I adore You and bow before You. You are worthy of praise. Hallelujah to Your name!" Thank Him today for the high privilege of praise. Review past memory work. No new memory verse today.

DAY FOURTEEN: Read Psalm 67:3-5

Today our word is *tehillah* which means "to sing a *hallal*." Sing your favorite praise hymn, meditating carefully on the words. Remember how important singing is in praising God. Determine to sing to God today with joyful heart. Review memory work. No new memory verse today.

DAY FIFTEEN: Read Psalm 72:18,19

Today our word is *yadah* which means "to praise with hands extended." Speak with God with your hands raised to Him. Say to Him, "Thy lovingkindness is better than life. My lips shall praise You; thus will I bless You. I will lift up my hands unto Your name." As you lift your hands to Him, meditate on what it means to thus extend your hands. Review memory work.

DAY SIXTEEN: Read Psalm 84:11,12

Today our word is *barak* which means "to bless." What a thought to entertain today that you and I can *bless* the Lord! Speak to Him a blessing. "Lord, I bless You with all that is within me. I bless Your name because Yours is the greatness, power, glory, majesty, splendor. I bless You because everything in earth and heaven is Yours. I bless You because Yours is the kingdom and You are exalted as head over all" (from 1 Chronicles 29:11). David blessed the Lord and so can you! Meditate on the thought that it is one thing to be blessed by the Lord but quite another to bless the Lord! For other words which bless the Lord, read Revelation 5:12-13. Determine to *barak* (bless) the Lord all through the day today.

DAY SEVENTEEN: Read Psalm 30:1-12

Our word today is *zamar* which means "to sing or to praise the Lord with a song." It is contained twice in this passage. In verse 4, "Sing [*zamar*] to the Lord, you saints of his; praise his holy name." It occurs again in verse 12, "that my heart may sing [*zamar*] to you and not be silent." I want you to sing a spiritual song today. That is simply a song which is not a psalm sung to the Lord. My song this morning is:

I love You Lord, and I lift my voice,
To worship You, O my soul, rejoice;
Take joy, my King, in what You hear,
May it be a sweet, sweet sound in Your ear.

If you do not know the tune to this one, either make up your own tune or sing out loud one you do know. Sing it through more than once or until the message goes through your heart to the Lord. Review memory work.

DAY EIGHTEEN: Read Psalm 95:1-7.

Our word today is *todah* which means "to give thanks." Today is a day for special thanksgiving. Begin right where you are and give thanks for things you normally take for granted: air and lungs with which to breathe it; lovely sights and eyes with which to see them; delicious fragrances and a sense of smell with which to enjoy them; life and the deep, inner feeling with which to savor it. Praise Him for something which has never, to your memory, been an object of thanksgiving. Have you ever given thanks for your thumb? It would be difficult to get a grip on anything without your thumb! How about your big toe? Terribly unappreciated but vital to standing and walking! Thank Him for a heart that pumps night and day without ever turning off. Bless Him for the bodily functions, hundreds of them, without which, life would be insupportable. You will discover a basic need in your life to practice the *attitude of gratitude* and thus will find it enjoyable and fulfilling. This will be a special day of praise as you practice thanksgiving. A wonderful song is centered around Psalm 100:4:

I will enter His gates with thanksgiving in my heart,
I will enter His courts with praise;
I will say "This is the day that the Lord has made!"
I will rejoice for He has made me glad.
He has made me glad, He has made me glad;
I will rejoice for He has made me glad.
He has made me glad, He has made me glad;
I will rejoice for He has made me glad.

Sing that song, whether you know the tune or not. The second time through, make it to God directly—"You have made me glad," etc.

DAY NINETEEN: Read Psalm 117

Our final word for praise is *shabach* which means "to shout or address in a loud voice." In Psalm 63:3 we found the Psalmist saying, "My lips shall praise [*shabach*] thee" (KJV). In Psalm 117 both *hallal* and *shabach* appear. "Praise [*hallal*] the Lord, all you nations; extol [*shabach*] him, all you peoples." There are several words for *shout* in the Hebrew language. It is a valid and indispensable form of praise. We may shout because of a victory made visible. We may shout in order to make a victory which has been promised come to fruition. Make the shout one of substance. In other words, don't just say, "Glory to God! Hallelujah!" Finish the shout of praise with a reason. "Glory to God because You are good and love me with such a great love! Hallelujah to You because Your faithfulness endures forever!"

DAY TWENTY: Read Luke 1:46-55

The remainder of our readings will be in the New Testament. Today we will join Mary in her praise song. As you read the reasons she lists for praising the Lord, meditate on the manner in which God has revealed Himself to you in these same areas. Be reminded that Christ is being formed in you (Galatians 4:19). Today make the commitment that Mary made earlier on when she said, "May it be to me as you have said." (Luke 1:38). Praise assumes that kind of commitment. As you make Mary's song your song, make Mary's commitment yours as well. Are you taking notes on your praise time? If not, begin taking notes today and review some of the previous days of praise. Continue reviewing previous memory work.

DAY TWENTY-ONE: Luke 1:67-79

Today we are witnessing Zechariah's song. Mark the reasons for this song contained in the verses of the passage. Make them your words of praise for what God has done. Recount promises that God has made to you and kept. Simply relate to Him your heartfelt gratitude for His faithfulness to do what He said He would. Talk to Him as you would a friend who has been faithful to you through the years. Continue to review memory verses.

DAY TWENTY-TWO: Read Luke 2:29-38

Today we observe the praise responses of Simeon and Anna. Since you and I have seen much more than they saw, then we should praise the Lord much more. Sing Julia Ward Howe's nineteenth-century hymn:

Mine eyes have seen the glory
of the coming of the Lord;
He is trampling out the vintage where
the grapes of wrath are stored;
He hath loosed the fateful lightning
of His terrible swift sword;
His truth is marching on.

Glory! glory, hallelujah! Glory, glory, hallelujah!
Glory, glory, hallelujah! Our God is marching on!

Review Simeon and Anna's reasons for praising the Lord and add your own. Especially praise God that there is clear evidence in history of His determination to fulfill every promise He has made. Praise the Lord. Review previous memory verses.

DAY TWENTY-THREE: Read Luke 10:17-24

Today we observe the praise life of Jesus. To be like Jesus is to praise! The reason for His praise is clear. He was rejoicing that God had revealed the things of the life of victory to His childlike followers. But He was also rejoicing that God had hidden the same things to those who were wise and learned! Look about you today and rejoice that the same thing is taking place. Repeat the words of Jesus when He said, "I praise you, Father, Lord of heaven and earth, because you have hidden these things from the wise and learned and revealed them to little children." Ask Him in the midst of praise to make you childlike in your love for Him. Review previous memory verses.

DAY TWENTY-FOUR: Read Matthew 6:9-13

We use the Lord's Prayer, calling it our Model Prayer, in our praises today. The prayer Jesus gave us as a model for our praying opens and closes with praise. "Our Father in heaven, hallowed [holy] be your name," is an address which opens the prayer. God's exalted position and His awesome name are objects of praise. "...For yours is the kingdom and the power and the glory forever. Amen." Frame your whole prayer time today in praise by opening and closing it in praises as Jesus suggested in the Model Prayer. You know that prayer by heart. Say it slowly and allow God to show you what the prayer means. Let these words sink into your heart, saying them over and over again, "yours is the kingdom and the power and the glory forever. Amen." Review previous memory verses.

DAY TWENTY-FIVE: Read Revelation 4:8-11

The remainder of our praise Scriptures will be taken from the Book of Revelation. We join the four creatures today who offer praises to God on the throne. Picture yourself before that throne joining them. Memorize Revelation 4:8*b*, "Holy, holy, holy is the Lord God Almighty, who was, and is, and is to come." Say it aloud until it sinks in. Remember the four creatures of Isaiah 6 whose praises were similar, "Holy, holy, holy is the Lord Almighty; the whole earth is full of his glory." Remember El Shaddai? It means "the God who nourishes, who is always sufficient, the almighty one." Celebrate the Almighty God today! Review previous memory work.

DAY TWENTY-SIX: Read Revelation 5:11-14

We join the millions of the hosts of heaven encircling the throne today. Try to imagine how many are involved. What is the greatest crowd you have ever witnessed? It surely will not compare to "thousands upon thousands, and ten thousand times ten thousand!" Memorize verse 12, the text of their praise: "Worthy is the Lamb who was slain, to receive power and wealth and wisdom and strength and honor and glory and praise!" Observe the seven things He is worthy to receive and recount them, saying them out loud to Him. Review yesterday's memory verse and add it to today's, quoting them both aloud to God. You are getting in practice for that great coming day!

DAY TWENTY-SEVEN: Read Revelation 11:15-18

Observe the announcement in verse fifteen: "The kingdom of the world has become the kingdom of our Lord and of his Christ, and he will reign for ever and ever." That day is surely coming! Take a minute to praise God for that day. Memorize verse 17. Link it to the memory verses on day twenty-five and twenty-six. Review previous memory work.

DAY TWENTY-EIGHT: Read Revelation 12:10-12

We observe "the beginning of the end" of the devil and his evil angels. We praise God today because we are overcomers through the blood, the testimony, and ultimate commitment. The devil is a defeated foe! The Holy Spirit was sent to share that glorious fact with us, "Of judgment, because the prince of this world is judged" (John 16:11, KJV). We praise God today in the victory declared, demonstrated, and delivered to us. Memorize 1 John 5:4, "For everyone born of God overcomes the world. This is the victory that has overcome the world, even our faith." Confess to God that passage: "I have been born of God. I have overcome the world. My faith is the victory which overcomes the world! Hallelujah!" Review previous passages for memory.

DAY TWENTY-NINE: Read Revelation 15:3,4 and Revelation 16:5-7

Memorize verse 3, "Great and marvelous are Your deeds, Lord God Almighty. Just and true are Your ways, King of the ages!" We are coming nearer and nearer to the end of all things pertaining to time. Our praises are growing! It is in order that we be prepared to join the great praise choirs of heaven. Imagine what it will be like then. Hallelujah! Review previous memory work.

DAY THIRTY: Read Revelation 19:1-8

Memorize Revelation 19:6*b*,7, "Hallelujah! For our Lord God Almighty reigns. Let us rejoice and be glad and give him glory! For the wedding of the Lamb has come, and his bride has made herself ready." We have at least four reasons to shout "Hallelujah!" We can say, "Hallelujah, salvation is complete! Hallelujah, the judgment of God on wickedness is consummated! Hallelujah, the reign of our God is confirmed! Hallelujah, the union of Christ with His Bride has come!"

Appendix E

Other References for Hebrew Words of Praise

Other Uses of *Hallal* in the Old Testament

2 Samuel 22:4; 1 Chronicles 16:10,25,36; 23:5,30; 25:3; 29:13; 2 Chronicles 7:6; 8:14; 20:19,21; 29:30; 30:21; 31:2; Ezra 3:11; Nehemiah 5:13; 18:3; 22:22,23; 26; 35:18; 48:1; 63:5; 69:30,34; 74:21; 102:18; 104:35 (Hallelujah); Psalm 105:45 (Hallelujah); Psalm 106:1,48 (Hallelujah); Psalm 107:32; 109:30; Psalm 111:1 (Hallelujah); Psalm 112:1 (Hallelujah); Psalm 113:1,9, (Hallelujah); Psalm 115:18 (Hallelujah); Psalm 116:19 (Hallelujah); Psalm 117:2 (Hallelujah); Psalm 119:175; 135:1,3,21 (Hallelujah); Psalm 145:2,3; 146:1,2,10 (1, 10—Hallelujah); Psalm 147:1,12,20 (12,20—Hallelujah); Psalm 148:1,2,3,4,5,7, 13,14 (1,14—Hallelujah); Psalm 149:1,3,9 (1,9—Hallelujah); Psalm 150:1,2,3,4,5,6 (Hallelujah); Isaiah 62:8-9; Jeremiah 20:13; Joel 2:26.

There are other uses of ***Hallal*** which do not pertain to praise of God. These have deliberately been omitted.

Other Uses of *Yadah* in the Old Testament (translated "praise")

Genesis 49:8; 2 Chronicles 7:3,6; Psalm 7:17; 28:7; 30:9; 33:2; 42:5,11; 43:4,5; 44:8; 45:17; 49:18; 52:9; 54:6; 57:9; 67:3,5; 71:22; 76:10; 86:12; 88:10; 89:5; 99:3; 108:3; 109:30; 111:1; 118:19,21,28; 119:7; 138:1,2,4; 142:7; Isaiah 12:1,4; 25:1; 38:18,19; Jeremiah 33:11.

Other Uses of *Barak* in the Old Testament Related to Praise to God

Genesis 9:26; 14:20; 24:27; Exodus 18:10; 1 Samuel 25:32,39; 2 Samuel 18:28; 1 Kings 1:48; 5:7; 8:15,56; 10:9; 1 Chronicles 16:36; 2 Chronicles 2:12; 6:4; 9:8; Ezekiel 7:27; Psalm 16:7; 18:46; 26:12; 28:6; 31:21; 34:1; 66:8,20; 68:26; 72:18-19; 89:52; 100:4b; 103:1,2,20,21,22; 104:1,35; 106:48; 115:18; 119:12; 124:6; 134:1,2; 135:19,20,21; 144:1; 145:1,2,10,21

Other Uses of *Tehillah* in the Old Testament

Psalm 9:14; 22:25; 33:1; 34:1; 35:28; 40:3; 48:10; 51:15; 65:1; 66:2,8; 71:6,8,14; 78:4; 79:13; 100:4; 102:21; 106:2,12,47; 109:1; 111:10; 119:171; 145:21; 147:1; 148:14; 149:1; Isaiah 42:8,10,12; 43:21; 48:9; 60:6,18; 61:11; 62:7; 63:7; Jeremiah 13:11; 17:14; 33:9; 49:25; Habakkuk 3:3; Zephaniah 3:19-20

Other Uses of *Zamar* in the Old Testament

Judges 5:3; 2 Samuel 22:50; Psalm 7:17; 9:2,11; 18:49; 21:13; 27:6; 30:4,12; 33:2; 47:6,7; 57:7,9; 61:8; 66:2,4; 68:4,32; 71:22,23; 75:9; 98:4,5; 101:1; 104:33; 105:2; 108:1,3; 135:3; 138:1; 144:9; 146:2; 147:7; 149:3; Isaiah 12:5

Other Uses of *Todah* in the Old Testament

Leviticus 22:29; 2 Chronicles 29:31; 33:16; Nehemiah 12:27,31,38,40; Psalm 26:7; 69:30; 107:22; 116:17; Isaiah 51:3; Jeremiah 17:26; 33:11; Amos 4:5

BIBLIOGRAPHY

Kittel, Gerhard and Friedrich, Gerhard, eds. *Theological Dictionary of the New Testament.* Grand Rapids: Wm. B. Eerdman's Publishing Co., 1976.

Kraybill, Donald. *The Upside Down Kingdom.* Scottdale, PA: Herald Press, 1978.

Vine, W.E. and Unger, Merrill F. and White, William, eds. *Vine's Complete Expository Dictionary of Old and New Testament Words*, New York: Thomas Nelson, 1985.

Wolf, Herbert. *An Introduction to the Old Testament Pentateuch.* Chicago: Moody Press, 1991.

Fulfill the desires of your heart

God planted dreams in you for a reason – your dreams really can come true!

There is no better Biblical story for understanding the process of seeing your dreams fulfilled than the life of Joseph. Doug Murren takes you to the heart of seeing your dreams fulfilled.

This inspiring book will renew and refresh you to pursue your dreams. With *Achieving Your Dreams – The Joseph Factor*, your dreams really can come true.

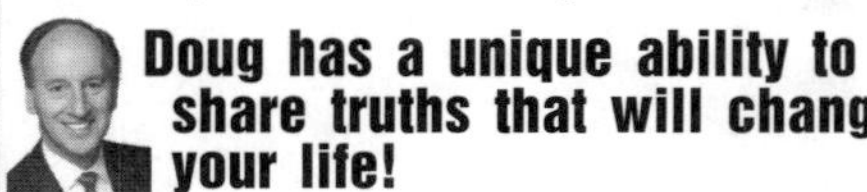

Doug has a unique ability to share truths that will change your life!

"Doug is one of today's finest young pastors/leaders and writers. He is uniquely gifted with an ability to capture the timelessness of truth and press it to the soul of today's circumstances to answer hurt or to beget hope–or both!" – Jack Hayford, Senior Pastor, The Church on the Way

A great book for all of us who dream big dreams

"The world scoffs at dreamers. God doesn't. He speaks to them. Doug Murren has written a practical, relevant book for all of us who want to dream big dreams for God and see them through."

– Michele Buckingham, Managing Editor, Ministries Today Magazine

Achieving Your Dreams by Doug Murren

ISBN: 1-883906-35-0 **Only $9.97**

Code # FIRE107

Worship can be the most exciting thing in your life!

Join Robert Webber on the journey in this book. Your worship will never be the same.

You'll discover hidden treasure in this fascinating look at Scripture. You'll find yourself and your church in the journey Dr. Webber paints for you.

No one can help you understand true worship in its rich historical context better than Robert Webber. He takes you on a journey into the very presence of God.

This book will help you experience the presence of God

"I highly recommend Worship: Journey into His Presence; *this book will help the reader connect with the presence of God and increase your interaction with Jesus.* – LaMar Boschman, Author and Dean of The Worship Institute.

Experience the fullness of worship

"Robert Webber helps us realize that worship is more than an inviting concept or an effective technique. It is a journey towards God's presence, into God's presence, and then–through God's presence–toward effective ministry in the world. – Jack Taylor, President of Dimensions Ministries, and author of *Hallelujah Factor.*

Worship: Journey Into His Presence by Robert Webber

ISBN: 1-883906-31-8 **Only $9.97**

Code # FIRE107

Available at your local Christian bookstore or call toll free (800) 597-1123

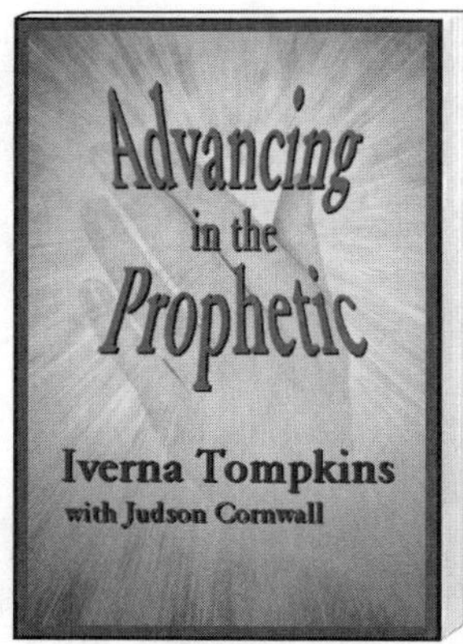

Advanced prophetic training –

This book is fresh, unique, and very insightful. You can unleash the fullness of the prophetic! You'll receive advanced prophetic training. Tompkins unearths powerful truths from the counselors in the book of Job. This book will give you fresh insight on personal prophecy and the prophetic.

You'll learn:

How to respond to prophecy
How to stir up the prophetic
How to refine truth from prophecy
How to recognize the living word in prophecy
How to reap from prophecy

Experience a fresh release of the prophetic in your life!

"Iverna has been used once again by God to bring encouragement to the body of Christ. She shows us how God uses the prophet and the prophetic word to keep us focused and to encourage us through His process."

– Jane Hansen, International President, Women's Aglow Fellowship

"Iverna Tompkins amazingly uses the life of Job to give us life-giving truths concerning prophets, prophetic ministry and God's process in perfecting His people."

– Bill Hamon, President, Christian International

Advancing in the Prophetic

by Iverna Tompkins/Judson Cornwall

ISBN: 1-883906-36-9 **Only $9.97**

Code # FIRE107

Change Your Money Stream –

Learn why money flows to some people and away from others

"This is the best financial teaching I've ever heard. I've used these principles for years. Finally, someone who teaches them from the Bible."

- Johnny Berguson, President of Kingdom, Inc. (Listed by *Inc. Magazine* as one of America's 500 fastest growing companies)

This is arguably the best financial book ever written. Mallonee goes to the root of finances. He explains from the Bible why money flows to some people and away from others.

Whether you have $5, $50, or $100,000, the Biblical principles in *Foolproof Finances* will work for you. These proven principles will help you get out of debt, or flourish when you're already doing well. This book will help anyone significantly improve their finances. Discover how you can be financially free.

Hardcover

Foolproof Finances by David Mallonee

ISBN: 1-883906-11-3 **Only $14.97**

Code # FIRE107

Available at your local Christian bookstore or call toll free (800) 597-1123

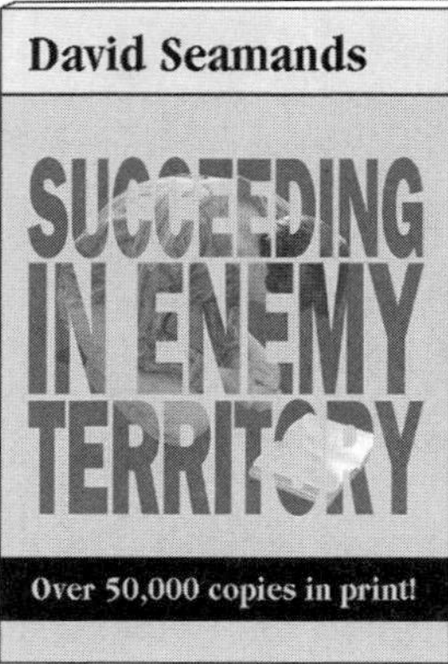

Discover the keys to succeeding in enemy territory!

You can not only succeed in enemy territory but you can thrive! This is your potential – you can not only win the battle for your life and mind, but tear down the fortresses of the enemy. You can truly succeed in enemy territory!

You'll learn:

How to live in victorious confidence
Five steps to resisting Satan's attacks
How to restore a broken past
How your weakest point can become your strongest
How to win the toughest battle you'll ever face

Brilliant! This book really will help you pursue your dreams!

"Succeeding in Enemy Territory, *from start to finish, is a brilliant balance of personal testimony, pertinent historical illustrations, and the foundation of the Biblical drama of Joseph all working together to drive you to dream on. What a reassurance to all of us to pursue our dreams!"*

– Jack Taylor, President of Dimension Ministries and author of the *Hallelujah Factor*

"This book gives new hope and encouragement..." – Dr. Norman Wright, counselor, seminar speaker, and best-selling author

Succeeding in Enemy Territory
by David Seamands

ISBN: 1-883906-34-2 **Only $9.97**

Code # FIRE107

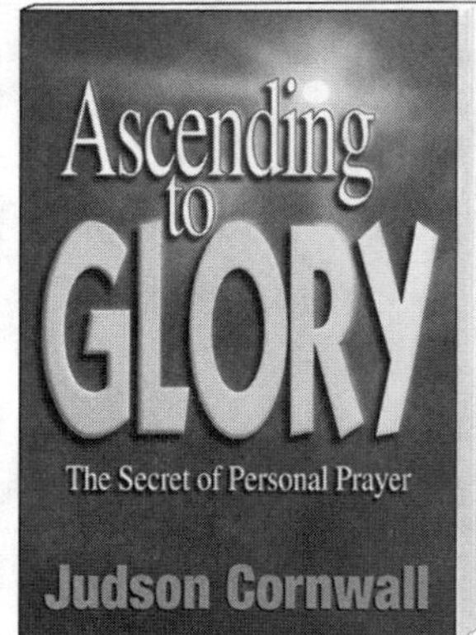

Experience Glorious Prayer –

Keys to effective prayer and intercession

No one is more qualified to write this book than Judson Cornwall!

"I know no one more qualified to write the book on Ascending to Glory *than Dr. Judson Cornwall. His life is lived in the secret of personal prayer because prayer is his way of life."*

–Dr. Fuschia Pickett,
Leading author and conference speaker

Discover the best part of prayer

"Practical illustrations from his own prayer life will awaken and direct the passion of your own pursuit of God. Above all, don't stop until you've worked your way to the very last chapter, because Judson truly has saved the best for last — the exhilarating pinnacle of loving embrace and intimacy with God."

–Bob Sorge,
Teacher and author

Ascending to Glory will lift your heart into the very presence of God. You'll discover nine ascending levels of prayer that will revolutionize your prayer and intercession. Rise into the very presence of God and experience glorious excursions into the heavenlies.

Ascending to Glory by Judson Cornwall

ISBN: 1-883906-32-6 **Only $9.97**

Code # FIRE107

Available at your local Christian bookstore or call toll free (800) 597-1123

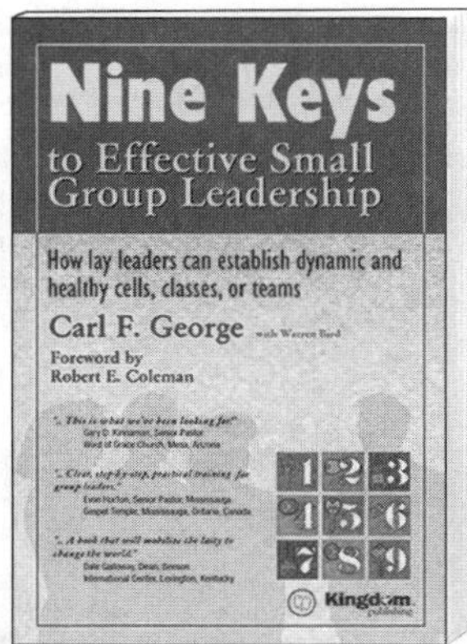

Be a more effective small group, Sunday school, or cell group leader!

Discover the nine Biblical keys that make you a more effective small group leader. You can propel small groups to new levels of fruitfulness for Christ.

Lead successful groups full of energy and life. Every small group will thrive as these scriptural keys are applied.

The Best Book on Small Groups!

"This is the best explanation in print of how God works through small groups... If I were a pastor, I would buy a copy of this book for every Sunday school teacher, small group leader, deacon, elder, staff member... every leader in my church. Then I'd buy a copy for the next set of leaders who will be produced when people get a hold of these nine keys."

– Reggie McNeal, Director of Leadership Development Team, South Carolina Baptist Convention, Columbia, SC

Carl George has been called on by congregations and leaders in 100 denominations to help them increase their effectiveness in ministry.

His writings are endorsed by leaders such as:

- **Bill Hybels**
- **Bill Bright**
- **Lyle Schaller**
- **Ralph Neighbour, Jr.**
- **Robert Coleman**
- **John Maxwell**
- **David Yonggi Cho**
- **Elmer L. Townes**

Nine Keys to Effective Small Group Leadership by Carl F. George

ISBN: 1-883906-13-X **Only $12.97**

Code # FIRE107

Available at your local Christian bookstore or call toll free (800) 597-1123

Make your small group grow and flourish!

Attention: Pastors, Small group leaders, Sunday School teachers, and cell leaders!

Effective leadership requires training and outstanding resources – *Small Group Audio Magazine™* is your answer. It will enable you to lead small groups full of energy and life – small groups that thrive. Each cassette features a message by one of the world's leading authorities on small groups along with exclusive interviews, helpful tips, and more!

Move to new levels of fruitfulness for Christ with *Small Group Audio Magazine!*

"The best thing about Small Group Audio Magazine *is the quality of the speakers. They know about small groups, based on their knowledge of Scripture and experience. They are not speaking from a theological viewpoint, but from their success… you can't argue with fruit!"* – Steve Roy, NH

The best of *Small Group Audio Magazine:*

- 12 audio cassettes featuring the world's foremost authorities on small groups and small group leadership
- 12 listening guides (one for each tape)
- A deluxe storage binder that stores all 12 cassettes and listening guides

Only ~~$97~~ $87 with coupon or special code on coupon + $9.97 shipping

60 Day Money Back Guarantee

Call toll free (800) 597-1123

With this coupon, you can get the best of *Small Group Audio Magazine* for only $87!

Just mention special Code # FIRE107 *to receive your $10 off!*

#AMBG

1-800-597-1123 P.O. Box 486 Mansfield, PA 16933

How to thrive even in chaos!

Discover how you can avoid "paradigm shock"

Change is a part of life. However, shifting paradigms can make you feel overwhelmed and out of control. Whether you're a pastor, church leader, small group leader, Sunday school teacher, or other lay leader you need to be able to manage change successfully.

Learn to anticipate change, cushion transitions, and redirect focus. Find out why even crisis-initiated changes do not have to be negative.

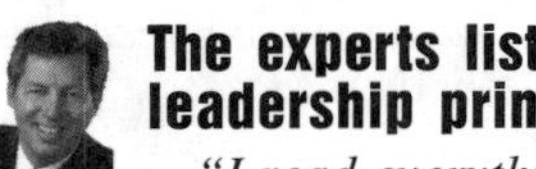

The experts listen to his leadership principles

"I read everything that Doug writes. Why? Because he is a pastor with an effective hand on today and a leader's eye on tomorrow. What he writes about works."

– John Maxwell, Author of bestselling books including *Developing the Leader Within You*

"...Pastor Doug Murren gives you answers you can begin to implement immediately."

– C. Peter Wagner, Author and Professor of Church Growth, Fuller Theological Seminary

Leadershift by Doug Murren

ISBN: 1-883906-30-X **Only $9.97**

Code # FIRE107

Discover how ordinary Christians can multiply the effectiveness of their whole church!

"This book was so good I could hardly put it down. This book showed me how to do everything... plus it's an abundant source of ideas. I thank God for putting this book in my hands. And I truly believe cassette ministry is a God given tool..."

– Carol Faust, Florida

As you catch the vision for cassette ministry, you'll quickly discover how to help make your entire church more effective through cassette ministry.

That's right. Anyone, anywhere can help make their ENTIRE church more effective through cassette ministry. You won't find another book like this anywhere!

The Comprehensive Guide to Cassette Ministry is loaded with practical ideas that will help you increase the effectiveness of nearly every ministry in your church. You'll discover four compelling Biblical reasons to do cassette ministry, the right – and wrong – ways to do it; how to fund your tape ministry; how to increase evangelism, teaching, and pastoral care through cassettes. You'll learn everything you could possibly want to know.

This book is helping ordinary Christians everywhere help make their entire church more effective!

The Comprehensive Guide to Cassette Ministry by Johnny Berguson

ISBN: 1-883906-12 **Only $19.97**

Code # FIRE107

Available at your local Christian bookstore or call toll free (800) 597-1123

Discover the keys to effective prayer and intercession!

Intercessors, prayer warriors, and praying Christians everywhere are discovering prayer in a fresh, powerful way. *Prayer Audio Magazine*™ will catapult your prayer and intercession to new levels.

God desires to communicate intimately with you through prayer. Through *Prayer Audio Magazine* you can invite the world's leading authorities into your own home to help you pray with greater effectiveness.

Each audio cassette has been prayerfully developed to help you maximize your prayer life.

Be more effective. Be informed. Pray with greater fervency and power! Get the best of *Prayer Audio Magazine* today!

The best of Prayer Audio Magazine:

- 12 audio cassettes featuring the world's leading authorities on prayer and intercession – these are 12 of the best issues ever of *Prayer Audio Magazine*
- 12 helpful listening guides (one for each cassette)
- Deluxe storage binder stores all 12 cassettes and listening guides
- Exclusive interviews and more
- Noted speakers include: Judson Cornwall, C. Peter Wagner, and Eddie & Alice Smith

"Prayer Audio Magazine *challenges us to keep pressing in to God. It keeps us informed, and brings us together to bond in prayer...*"

– Pastor Jim Ottman, Maine

Only ~~$97~~ $87 with coupon or special code on coupon + $9.97 shipping

60 Day Money Back Guarantee

Call toll free (800) 597-1123

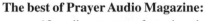

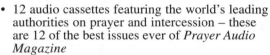

With this coupon, you can get the best of *Prayer Audio Magazine* for only $87!

Just mention special Code # FIRE107 *to receive your $10 off!*

 # AMBP

1-800-597-1123

P.O. Box 486
Mansfield, PA 16933

Actually experience the most powerful moves of God on the earth today

through *Renewal Audio Magazine*™!

"Renewal Audio Magazine *will keep you at the front row of what God is doing and saying in the earth today.*" – Bob Sorge,
Author of *The Fire of Delayed Answers*
(and many other books)

Advance to the forefront of what God is doing throughout the earth today with *Renewal Audio Magazine*.

You can experience what God is doing in your own living room, heart, and life. *Renewal Audio Magazine* harnesses the unique power of the cassette to take you where God is moving today. You'll feel God's heartbeat with an immediacy that will excite you.

Each cassette contains critical messages from some of the most anointed men and women on earth. These men and women have been specially anointed for this hour. You'll also hear exclusive interviews and much more. You'll find your spiritual life moving to new levels with each cassette!

Renewal Audio Magazine will both refresh and inspire you!

Call toll free (800) 597-1123

The best of Renewal Audio Magazine

- 12 of the best audio cassette issues ever of *Renewal Audio Magazine* – hear from some of the most anointed men and women of our generation
- 12 listening guides (one for each tape)
- Deluxe storage binder stores all cassettes and listening guides
- Exclusive interviews and more
- Noted speakers include Francis Frangipane, Bob Mumford, Mike Bickle, C. Peter Wagner, Iverna Tompkins, and Ed Silvoso

Only ~~$97~~ $87 with coupon or special code on coupon + $9.97 shipping

60 Day Money Back Guarantee

SAVE $10

With this coupon, you can get the best of *Renewal Audio Magazine* for only $87!

Just mention special Code # FIRE107 *to receive your $10 off!*

 # AMBR

1-800-597-1123 P.O. Box 486
Mansfield, PA 16933

Experience new depths in worship

Invite the world's leading authorities into your own home through *Worship Audio Magazine™*. Each cassette contains key messages, exclusive interviews, and more.

With the best of *Worship Audio Magazine*, you'll find yourself moving to new depths of insight and worship experience!

"...up-to-date spiritual manna...I am very pleased..." – Mike Kelly, Tennessee

"Worship Audio Magazine *has expanded my understanding... The messages are greatly complemented by the personal interviews."* – Karen Heller, New York

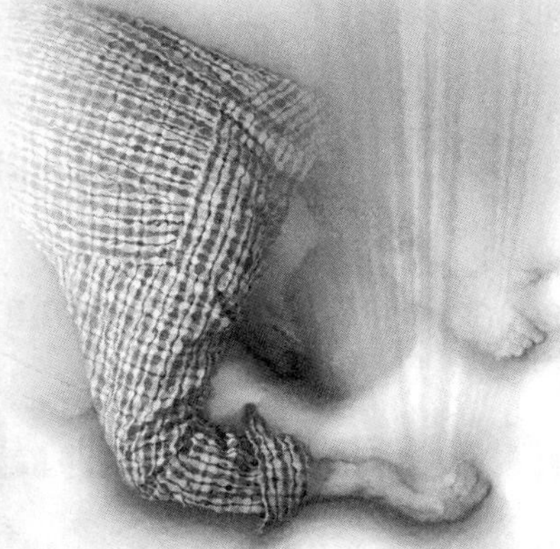

The best of *Worship Audio Magazine*:

- 12 of the best audio cassette issues ever of *Worship Audio Magazine* – hear from some of the most anointed men and women of our generation
- 12 listening guides (one for each tape)
- Deluxe storage binder stores all cassettes and listening guides
- Exclusive interviews and more
- Noted speakers include: Robert Webber, Judson Cornwall, LaMar Boschman, and Bob Mumford

Only ~~$97~~ $87 with coupon or special code on coupon + $9.97 shipping

60 Day Money Back Guarantee

Call toll free (800) 597-1123

SAVE $10

With this coupon, you can get the best of *Worship Audio Magazine* for only $87!

Just mention special Code # FIRE107 *to receive your $10 off!*

 # AMBW

1-800-597-1123 P.O. Box 486 Mansfield, PA 16933

Don't miss these exciting books from Kingdom Publishing!

Worship: Journey Into His Presence by Robert Webber
ISBN: 1-883906-31-8 **$9.9**

Achieving Your Dreams: The Joseph Factor by Doug Murren
ISBN: 1-883906-35-0 **$9.9**

Succeeding in Enemy Territory by David Seamands
ISBN: 1-883906-34-2 **$9.9**

Foolproof Finances by David Mallonee
ISBN: 1-883906-11-3 **$14.9**

Nine Keys to Effective Small Group Leadership by Carl George
ISBN: 1-883906-13-X **$12.9**

The Comprehensive Guide to Cassette Ministry by Johnny Berguson
ISBN: 1-883906-12 **$19.9**

The Classic℠ King James Version Bible on Cassette narrated by Dr. Vernon Lapps
ISBN: 1-883906-14-8 **$47.0**

Fire Wind imprint:

Ascending to Glory: The Secret of Personal Prayer by Judson Cornwall
ISBN: 1-883906-32-6 **$9.9**

Hallelujah Factor by Jack Taylor
ISBN: 1-883906-33-4 **$9.9**

Advancing in the Prophetic by Iverna Tompkins/Judson Cornwall
ISBN: 1-883906-36-9 **$9.9**

Available at your local Christian bookstore!

If you don't have a local Christian bookstore, you may call or write

Kingdom publishing **1-800-597-1123**

P.O. Box 486, Lambs Creek Road, Mansfield, PA 16933

http://www.kingdompub.com

* All prices subject to change without notice